18/10/10

12/3/13

D0854793

EDWARD MARSTON

John Christie

the national archives

First published in 2007 by
The National Archives
Kew, Richmond
Surrey, TW9 4DU, UK

www.nationalarchives.gov.uk

The National Archives

A catalogue card for this book is available from the British Library.

ISBN 978 1 905615 16 2

Cover illustration: John Christie and the 'murder house',
10 Rillington Place (MEPO 2/9535)
Jacket design and page typesetting by Goldust Design
Page design and plate section typesetting by Ken Wilson | point 918
Picture research by Gwen Campbell
Printed in Germany by
Bercker Graphischer Betreib GmbH & Co

Contents

—

Portrait of a Killer

John Christie was one of the most notorious killers of the twentieth century, murdering eight victims including a mother and child during a decade of destruction from 1943 to 1953. A serial killer is always reviled, but aspects of Christie's crimes particularly appalled 1950s Britain and continue to shock and fascinate in equal measure: his necrophilia and other sexual habits; his casual disposal of his victims' bodies in his house and garden; his cold-blooded assaults on women who knew and trusted him; the fact that he let an innocent man hang for his own crimes. It is hard to reconcile these acts with what we know of Christie's kindly, authoritative persona. This self-styled pillar of the community used a dead woman's thigh bone to prop up his garden fence, wore plimsolls stained by semen, and ate and slept near the decomposing bodies of his victims.

These horrifying scenarios were a world away from Christie's wholesome Yorkshire childhood, although aspects of his early life did suggest future trouble. John Reginald Halliday Christie was born on 8 April 1898 in Black Boy House, on the moors just outside Halifax. The family was dominated by his father, Ernest John Christie, a carpet designer by trade and a strict disciplinarian by nature. Christie's mother was a handsome woman who bore seven children: Percy, Florence, Winnie, Effie, Reggie (John) and Dolly, along with a fifth daughter who died as a baby. Christie therefore grew up in a largely female household. His father beat him for the most trivial offences and, because the lad was frail, his mother was over-protective towards him. Christie became shy, withdrawn and secretive.

School was a welcome escape from his domineering father. Excelling as a pupil, Christie won a scholarship to Halifax Secondary School where his special subject was mathematics. He had above-average intelligence, played games with enthusiasm and got on relatively well with his classmates. Because her younger son was her favourite child, his mother took delight in reading his glowing school reports.

When not at school, Christie helped his father in the garden, sang in the All Souls choir, was a scout in the church troop and eventually became assistant scoutmaster. The uniform gave him a sense of identity and authority, and he liked to wear it when he was not involved in scouting activities. This habit foreshadowed his later pleasure in wearing a police uniform.

Three events in Christie's childhood had a strong influence on his developing personality. The first occurred when he was eight: his maternal grandfather died and the boy was invited to view the corpse. As he had always been frightened of the old man, Christie went with trepidation, but the experience was a turning point in his life. He later described his feelings of fascination and pleasure as he looked at the lifeless body. The Christies had by now moved to a house in the Boothtown district of Halifax overlooking All Souls cemetery; Christie enjoyed playing among the gravestones and peering through a crack in a children's vault at the coffins. Death had an increasing allure for him.

As yet it held no sexual dimension, but another event that happened when he was nine or ten did. Christie was deeply embarrassed when a married sister lifted up her leg to fasten her shoe and exposed the leg up to the knee. To a small boy in the repressive world of Edwardian England, this was a sight that brought a blush to his cheek, and he did not forget it. Accustomed to being bullied by his sisters, he had also been unwittingly shocked by one of them.

The third event occurred after Christie left school at fifteen. He got a job as assistant cinema operator and enjoyed the work. After church one evening, he and some friends went for a walk down the Monkey Run, the local lovers' lane. They paired off in couples, but the girl with whom Christie found himself derided him for his sexual incompetence. Word of his failure was soon passed on and Christie had to endure taunts of 'Reggie-No-Dick' and 'Can't-Do-It-Christie'. The humiliation helped to crystallize his hatred, fear and resentment of the opposite sex.

In September 1916, at the age of 18, Christie enlisted in the army and was called up the following April to join the 52nd

Notts and Derby Regiment (The Sherwood Foresters). He was still slightly built, of average height and with pale gingery hair. Contemporaries remembered him as a cheerful, red-faced fellow who rarely grumbled; as he moved into manhood, it seems, Christie was still suppressing anger as he had learned to do as a child. In the extrovert world of the army, he could never be wholly at ease.

It was during this time that he began to visit prostitutes. Because he was paying for their services, his partners were submissive and unthreatening, and there was no danger that they would laugh at him or proclaim his sexual inadequacy to others. Given his background, Christie had to wrestle with guilt and shame: furtive couplings in squalid bedrooms were a world away from wholesome family life and regular attendance at church. No wonder his sexuality was tortured.

In April 1918, Christie's regiment was ordered overseas. On arrival in France, it was split up and seconded to various units in need of trained signalmen. Christie was attached to the Duke of Wellington's (West Riding) Regiment, serving behind the lines. At the end of June, a mustard gas shell exploded nearby and knocked him unconscious. Christie always claimed that he was blinded for several months and that he lost his voice for over three years.

There is no medical evidence, however, to support the claim of blindness and, though he did lose his voice for some weeks, he was discharged from a military hospital in Stoke as being fit for duty. According to the diagnosis, the loss of speech was not caused by gas poisoning but by functional aphonia brought on by fright. When he lost his voice again in March 1919, he went to a hospital in Newcastle and was again diagnosed as suffering from functional aphonia. After only four days of treatment, he was deemed fit once more for service.

Christie's voice was permanently affected by the incident in the trenches and he always spoke in a whisper. He told everyone about being gassed. Being wounded in action was more heroic than having a form of shell shock, and as proof of his claims he would point to the fact that when he was demobilized at the end of 1919, he was given a small disability pension. Christie thereafter used real or imaginary medical conditions to gain sympathy; these were among the first indications of a tormented personality.

Returning to Halifax, Christie took a job as a cinema operator, then became a clerk in Sutcliffe's wool mill. He began courting a neighbour, Ethel Simpson Waddington (see plate 11). A kind and compassionate young woman, she was also rather plain, passive, homely and unworldly. Christie detested the brazen females who tempted him and who were likely to expose his sexual shortcomings, and Ethel offered him safety from the kind of derision he had received in the Monkey Run.

In spite of his strong religious upbringing, the couple were married at Halifax Register Office on 10 May 1920. A measure of peace and contentment had finally come into his life. Christie later admitted that the marriage was not consummated for some time and that, at its best, intercourse between them was very spasmodic. As a result, there was little hope of Ethel's becoming pregnant. But she was patient and understanding. With a good job and a loving wife, Christie was enjoying a security he had never known before.

It was not enough for his restless spirit. Quitting the job at the mill, he became a postman, giving him another uniform behind which to hide. Off duty, he started to visit prostitutes again. On duty, he began stealing postal orders. It was some months before the thefts were discovered. Less than a year after marrying Ethel, he was sentenced to three months' imprisonment on each of three charges. It was a bitter blow to his wife and family. Ethel, however, stood by him.

After his release from prison, a curious incident occurred. At a function involving his family, his father reproached him for being so slow. Years of pent-up fury suddenly exploded. 'You bugger off!' Christie yelled at the man he had always feared, his voice miraculously regaining its full power. It did not last. During the following year, his speech was again reduced to a murmur. People who met him for the first time found his hoarse whisper unsettling.

Early in 1923, Christie faced the magistrates once more, charged with obtaining money by false pretences and with violent conduct. Bound over on the first charge, he was put on twelve months' probation for the second. Halifax was now an uncomfortable place for him. He had been disowned by his family and there were rumours about his association with prostitutes, while his criminal record made it difficult for him to find a job. Ethel suggested a new start in Sheffield, but the marriage was falling apart: after a spate of rows, Christie left his wife with relatives in Sheffield and headed for London.

Life in the capital got off to an inauspicious start. Christie was knocked down by a car and had an operation on his knee in hospital. His next collision was with the forces of law and order. In September 1924, he was sentenced at Uxbridge Petty Sessions to three and six months' consecutive imprisonment on two charges of larceny. At the time, he was of no fixed abode, and as the years rolled by he increasingly inhabited a sleazy world of pimps, prostitutes and other low company. By day, he might eke out a living as a clerk or a book-keeper; by night, he followed more desperate urges.

By 1929 he was living with a prostitute in Battersea. During a row, Christie seized her son's cricket bat and struck her on the head. He was sentenced to six months' hard labour for malicious wounding. The fierce regimentation of prison life was degrading. An obsessively private man was stripped of all privacy. Someone who had relished dressing up as a scout, soldier and postman was again at the mercy of men in uniform.

Whatever promises he made in prison about turning over a new leaf, he did not manage to keep. Back at Uxbridge Petty Sessions in 1933, he was charged with stealing a car from a

Roman Catholic priest who had befriended him. Christie came to the conclusion that he had to break the depressing cycle of arrest and conviction. He wrote to Ethel and asked her to live with him again on his release. Lonely, frustrated and now in her mid-thirties, Ethel had been leading a decidedly humdrum existence in Sheffield. She was offered companionship and the countenance of being married once more. After visiting Christie in prison, she agreed to go back to him.

It was a disastrous mistake, but it did not seem so at the time. Ethel set up house in Notting Hill while Christie turned his back on petty crime. He found a job as a ledger clerk, working hard and keeping up appearances, and he and Ethel learned to rub along together. But he had not renounced his former life: if his wife was visiting family in Sheffield, Christie consorted with prostitutes. It was a double life that would in time take on a much darker aspect.

In 1938, the Christies moved into 10 Rillington Place, occupying the ground-floor flat. The crumbling Victorian house was at the end of a terrace in a seedy cul-de-sac near Ladbroke Grove underground station (see plate 1). The noise from the trains was deafening and must have dominated everyday life. The Christies' shabby flat comprised a living room facing the street, a bedroom behind it looking into the small yard, and a kitchen (see plate 2). At the far end of the kitchen was an alcove used for storing coal. Next to this was a wash-house only accessible from the yard. There was no bathroom and the outside lavatory served everyone in the house. The Christies had the use of the garden.

The long-standing tenant of the first-floor flat, which also consisted of three rooms, was Charles Kitchener, a retired railwayman with failing eyesight. The Christies saw very little of him. The smaller top-floor flat was temporarily unoccupied; it had a bed-sitting room at the front and a kitchen at the back. Although 10 Rillington Place had three floors, it was a cramped and neglected house with peeling stucco and years' worth of untouched grime. It was an ideal habitat for John Christie.

Though he stayed in work, he had been shifting jobs regularly. Events in Europe gave him an opportunity for more secure employment: replying to an advertisement from the London police force, he volunteered for the Emergency Reserve. Any check on his criminal record would have invalidated him but, incredibly, the check was never made. In 1939, Christie was enrolled as a special constable. He was back in uniform at last.

For four years, he operated out of Harrow Road police station, savouring the power and status of his position. He had regained some dignity. Zealous and efficient, he won two commendations for his 'ability relating to criminal offences', a phrase that later took on an ironic ring. Christie acquired a first aid certificate (he later used the manuals to pretend to a doctor's medical knowledge). His officiousness earned him a new nickname — 'the Himmler of Rillington Place'.

During the Blitz, Christie was in his element. As he helped

with rescue work, his fascination with dead bodies was intensified by the sight of the endless corpses he dug out of bombed houses. While pursuing looters and other criminals, he had the perfect excuse to enter the shadowy underworld which he had always had to access in secret before. Rewards were plentiful: he gratefully seized favours from prostitutes and bribes from criminals, relishing the chance to order people about. A police uniform was the perfect disguise. He used his privileged position to follow women, keeping notes of them for many years.

In 1943, he went too far. He began a relationship with a woman who worked at the police station. To an insecure man in his forties, it must have been exciting to have sex with a younger woman. When her soldier-husband returned from overseas, however, he heard the gossip and actually caught Christie with his wife. After beating him up, he flung Christie out of the house. There was clear evidence of adultery: years later, the husband divorced his wife by citing Christie as co-respondent.

Discovery with the woman was utterly humiliating, and the severe beating inflicted far more than mere physical pain on Christie: it caused untold psychological torment. In front of his lover, he had been revealed as weak, cowardly and unable to defend himself. His career as a policeman was threatened. If it ended, he could no longer strut about in uniform and trade on people's respect for his status. The life and work he had loved were in danger of being violently snatched away from him. Rage, bitterness and thwarted lust built up in him until he found a target.

---

CHAPTER ONE

10 Rillington Place

In 1939, at the age of 17, Ruth Fuerst, an Austrian student nurse, came to England and stayed after the outbreak of war. Four years later, she was working in a munitions factory in Davies Street and living in a single room in Oxford Gardens, only a short walk away from Rillington Place. As she was poorly paid at the factory, she took to part-time prostitution: her attractive looks — she was tall with dark brown hair — must have helped to attract clients, including Christie. In August 1943, Fuerst went to Christie's flat while his wife was away in Sheffield; it was not her first visit.

The Metropolitan Police files record Christie's account of the encounter:

> I got on the bed and had intercourse with her. While I was having intercourse with her, I strangled her with a rope… She was completely naked. I tried to put her clothes back on her. She had a leopard skin coat and I wrapped this around her. I took her from the bedroom and put her under the floor boards.
>
> (MEPO 2/9535; see plate 20)

As this indicates, Christie was untroubled by remorse, but concealing the crime became urgently important: a telegram arrived, warning Christie that Ethel would return that evening. After hiding the dead body under the floorboards in the front room, he quickly cleaned up the mess in the bedroom.

Braced to welcome his wife back home, Christie was distressed to see that she was accompanied by her brother, Henry Waddington. All three of them spent the night in the flat: Ethel and Christie in the bed on which Fuerst had been strangled and Waddington in the front room, unaware of the corpse beneath the floorboards. On the next day, when the other two had left, Christie reclaimed the body and clothing. After putting them in the wash-house (see plate 7), he dug a grave outside; neighbours who gave him a friendly wave thought he was simply gardening.

When it was dark that night, Christie told Ethel he was going to the lavatory. He then took the body from the wash-house and buried it along with the clothing. On the following day, when he was burning rubbish, he dug up the clothing and burned that as well. Of the murder itself, he had a vivid memory. 'I remember,' he later said, 'as I gazed down at the still form of my first victim, experiencing a strange, peaceful thrill' (Christie quotes from DPP 2/2246). Christie had begun the year as a policeman with missionary zeal. He ended it as a murderer and necrophile.

Having left the police of his own volition at the end of 1943, Christie took up civilian employment the following year at the Ultra Radio Works in Acton. It was there he befriended someone from the assembly line. Unlike most of the other women who attracted his interest, Muriel Eady was highly respectable. In her early thirties, she was short, stout and had dark brown hair. She lived with her aunt in Putney. Over lunch one day, Christie invited her to come to tea with her man friend to meet Ethel; the occasion went well and the couple visited the flat again. One evening, all four of them went to the cinema together.

Christie had already identified Eady as his next victim. 'I planned it all out very carefully,' he later confessed. But he had to bide his time. It was not until autumn that the right conditions finally presented themselves, when Ethel went off to visit her brother in Sheffield. By that time Christie had won Eady's confidence so completely that he was able to spin his murderous web. He enticed her to Rillington Place with the promise of curing the catarrh from which she was suffering with an inhalation device he had constructed. This device was not only the means of getting her there, it was also a way of subduing her; unlike the promiscuous Ruth Fuerst, Eady was sure to rebuff any sexual advances.

When she arrived at the flat, Eady was given a cup of tea to help her to relax, and invited to sit in Christie's strange deck-chair with rope strands instead of canvas. Christie then showed her his device. It was a square glass jar with a metal screw-top lid in which two holes had been made. Into one of these, he had fed a rubber tube. When Eady sniffed the other end of the tube, she inhaled Friar's Balsam; what she did not realize was that Christie had inserted another tube into the jar, attached to a gas point in the wall. When he released a bulldog clip on the second tube, coal gas was mixed with the heady aroma of Friar's Balsam. Breathing it in, Eady soon began to lose consciousness.

Christie's plan had worked perfectly. Carrying her to the bedroom, he removed her knickers, ravished her and strangled her with a rope in the process. She was defenceless. Looking at the body afterwards, he recalled, 'once again I experienced that quiet, peaceful thrill. I had no regrets.' After this second callous murder, he had more time to collect himself. He left the body in the wash-house for a while, then buried it in the garden, still exulting in what he saw as his triumph. Having deceived an innocent woman, he had killed her in the most bestial fashion, and what made it supremely satisfying was that—as in the case of Fuerst—he had got away with it. Nobody would suspect a polite, mild-mannered, contentedly married man of committing such appalling crimes.

Without knowing it, Christie had initiated a series of events that would turn 10 Rillington Place into the most notorious address in the country. When the chilling truth about these and other murders was finally revealed, the public reacted with a mixture of horror and disbelief. How could the diffident and intelligent young man from Halifax turn in middle age into a perverted serial killer? How could someone who had fought for his country in one war and served as a policeman during another behave like a monster? And at what stage did the idea of sex and death coalesce in his warped mind?

A number of factors were involved. The painful experiences in his early life obviously played their part (see plate 24): his family's treatment of him, including his mother's emasculating protectiveness, caused a dangerous build-up of suppressed anger, and as he revealed after his arrest for the murders, the Monkey Run incident had continued to preoccupy him. It seemed that apart from his mother, Christie could not love or trust any woman and came to despise the whole sex.

His marriage to Ethel Waddington, which could have been the making of a less troubled man, was doomed from the start, its failure another factor in Christie's deepening hatred of women. Whatever else Ethel offered him, it was not unbridled passion: their sex life was fitful and unsatisfying. Though she was very loyal to him, Ethel was not above taunting him about his failure to maintain an erection. Her main value was to offer a cloak of respectability. During their nine years apart, Christie had drifted from job to job, taken his pleasures in the arms of whores and committed crimes to help to pay for their services. With Ethel beside him, he abjured petty crime and had some focus back in his life. During her absences from London, however, he could return to his old haunts and vices.

The person that friends, neighbours and work colleagues saw was bald, bespectacled Reg Christie, plausible, reliable and harmless, a middle-class gentleman in a run-down working-class district of west London. He lacked charm and made a poor impression on people he met. Yet he could be kind and generous.

After a child was tragically killed in a fall, someone took up a collection. Most people contributed in pennies; Christie put half a crown into the tin.

The presence of a wife, outwardly happy, enabled Christie to masquerade as a decent, honest, loving husband, bravely enduring the ailments that troubled him on a regular basis and sent him to Dr Odess's surgery in Colville Square time and time again. He might have lost his scout's uniform and those he wore as a postman, a soldier and a policeman, but Ethel provided him with another uniform, that of a married man with no apparent ambitions beyond what he had already achieved. Wife, home and respectability—Christie had the holy trinity of social acceptance.

Yet this same man had buried two victims in the garden where he could be seen quietly working. He could sleep in a bed where both women had been brutally raped, strangled and gloated over. He could wave his wife off on holiday then visit prostitutes. Christie resented having to pay for sex, but it was the only way that he could indulge his wilder fantasies. The fact that he was compelled to depend on such women before he could reach ejaculation made him despise them even more. Strong evidence of masturbation suggests that he explored his fantasies when alone in Rillington Place.

The brutalizing effect of the Second World War cannot be underestimated. Having experienced warfare at first hand, he was grateful to be involved on the home front this time. During the daily bombardment of London, he would have been shepherding people in and out of air raid shelters, checking to see that the blackout was observed at night and keeping an eye out for any criminal activity. Death was all around him. The corpses he helped to unearth from bomb sites were often in a hideous condition, but he was intrigued rather than shocked. Not only did he handle the corpses of countless women killed during the Blitz, with his first aid skills he had licence to touch those who were wounded. The possibilities for a legitimate grope must have been unlimited.

Being appointed as a policeman had given him immense self-respect that had grown with the passing years. While upholding the law, he was, in a sense, above it and exploited his position to the full. What we see in the life of Christie is a slow escalation from petty crime and street-corner vice into dark perversions that eventually found their apogee in the merciless killing of Ruth Fuerst and Muriel Eady. In neither case had he acted on impulse. Cunning and calculation were at play. The heightened pleasure and sense of conquest he experienced during the murders was dizzying: it was only a matter of time before he would want to recapture the same incomparable thrill.

Before that could happen, Christie needed to find another victim. Fortune favoured him by providing him a potential target very close to home. At Easter 1948, Timothy and Beryl Evans moved into the second-floor flat at 10 Rillington Place.

London was a bleak and cheerless place at that time. The

aftermath of war had brought unrelieved austerity: bomb damage was everywhere, food was rationed and there were irksome fuel shortages. Citizens of the drab capital still had to carry identity cards. Delight at victory over Nazi Germany was tempered by a pervading sadness over the deaths of untold thousands of British soldiers who had perished in combat and the masses of civilians who had died during the Blitz.

Because there were no pollution laws, factories continued to belch out smoke unchecked, and smog was turning into a more subtle killer than the Luftwaffe. The city had a jaded, unhealthy air: houses were dirty and unpainted, streets were dimly lit at night, and in the world of rented accommodation, there was a strong whiff of poverty.

Rillington Place and its environs were, to some extent, emblematic of all that was wrong with the capital. But the flat was all that Timothy and Beryl Evans could afford. It was their first real home. Married for barely six months, they had been living with Evans's mother and stepfather in nearby St Mark's Road. Beryl was made to feel like one of the family but, when she became pregnant, it was obvious that the little house could not accommodate a baby as well. It was Evans's sister Eileen who first spotted the sign outside 10 Rillington Place through the window of a train to Ladbroke Grove, as it passed above the north side of the cul-de-sac. When she gave the details to her brother, she unwittingly set tragedy in motion.

THE BOY FROM WALES

Timothy John Evans was born on 20 November 1924 in a terraced house on a street called Mount Pleasant, in Merthyr Vale. This grubby mining village in South Wales was surrounded by slag heaps; the street was probably far from pleasant. Evans's father Daniel was a coal haulier who deserted the family before his son's birth, leaving his wife Thomasina to cope with her three-year-old daughter Eileen and the new baby. In 1929 she married Penry Probert, who was also employed in the coal industry. Later that year, she gave birth to a third child, Maureen.

Timothy Evans was a backward boy. He could not speak properly until the age of five and had serious learning difficulties at school. After only a couple of years, his education came to a sudden halt. He was bathing one day in the River Taff when he cut his left foot on broken glass; the wound was tied with a dirty handkerchief and soon became infected. By the time it was examined by a doctor, it was too late: Evans had a tubercular verruca on his foot that would never heal. Year after year, he was in and out of hospital. On the rare occasions when he had schooling, he floundered badly.

In the boisterous world of childhood, Evans became an outsider. He lacked the fitness and energy to join in robust games and his low intelligence was a source of mockery among the other pupils. He was a thin, pale, undersized boy with a bad foot surrounded by stocky lads from mining families. Sickly, isolated and illiterate, Timothy Evans had an unhappy boyhood.

When the Depression hit the coalfields in the early thirties, his stepfather, like so many others, found himself out of work. Probert searched for employment in London. He found a job as a painter and decorator in 1935, and the family moved to Notting Hill. It was a bewildering experience for Evans. Having grown up in a modest house in the valley he was now thrust into a vast city, where the scale and the pace of everything took his breath away. In a small Welsh community, he had known virtually everyone. Now he was lost amid a multitude of strangers, more of an outsider than ever.

He attended St Francis' Roman Catholic School in Portland Road but his stay was short-lived: the condition of his foot worsened and he went into hospital, remaining there for nine months. As a result of an outbreak of measles in the children's ward, Mrs Probert was asked to remove her son before he caught the disease. When she tried to do so, however, Evans protested so much that she had to leave him there for another week. After that, he consented to be taken away from the hospital and was wheeled home in an old pram. The little invalid was eleven years old.

Throughout the following year, he was a regular outpatient at the hospital, but his foot continued to trouble him. There were times when it swelled up so badly that he was unable to put on his shoe. On other occasions, his whole leg ballooned up and he was forced to retire to bed. Because of his disability, he made few friends in London and in 1937 he asked if he could go back to Wales, where he felt he belonged. After discussion with her husband, Mrs Probert agreed to let him go, feeling that a change of scene might do him good. Evans duly went off by train to live with his grandmother in Merthyr Vale.

When his foot improved, he was able to return to school and meet up with old friends. The fact that he had lived in London must have impressed the other lads, many of whom had never been outside Wales, and Evans no doubt regaled them with stories about his adventures in the capital. These stories were based much more on imagination than fact: Evans was an accomplished liar, a boastful youth who invented a rich fantasy life to compensate for the miserable one that he actually lived. His lies were both a defence mechanism and a means of gaining attention.

Evans still struggled at school. Finding it difficult to concentrate, he fell even further behind his classmates. Though he could not read, he enjoyed looking at comics where everything was explained pictorially. But while the other boys committed themselves joyfully to the rough and tumble of rugby, Evans was once again excluded. His uncle, Mr Lynch, who also lived in Mount Pleasant, claimed that the lad was only happy when hunting rats down a stokehold (coal bunker). Being back among his own people had not given Evans the reassurance he sought.

When he left school, he got a job at the local mine. Evans was now a man in a working world, but the illusion was only temporary. The infection in his foot flared up again and he was forced once more to go into hospital. In London, his anxious mother received regular bulletins about his condition: when there had been no improvement after a couple of months, she brought him back to Notting Hill.

After a visit to a local doctor, Evans was sent first to St Charles' Hospital and then to the Moorland Clinic for Tubercular Children at Alton in Hampshire, where he stayed for a year. Finally given the specialized treatment he needed, there was slow but noticeable progress. Evans, however, must have felt frustrated to be a full-time patient once again. He was a moody, excitable Welsh lad with a quick temper and a runaway tongue, but instead of being out in the real world he was kept in a ward filled with young children who had serious tubercular conditions. He took refuge once more in vivid fantasies.

When he was released from hospital, Evans rejoined his family in Cornwall Road, an address to which they had moved in 1938. Glad to leave the Moorland, he was nevertheless aware of how effective his treatment there had been. His foot would always be deformed, making him walk with a slight limp, but he never had to endure the same crises in his health again. The war was now at its height and he soon became accustomed to the pandemonium of the Blitz with its blaring air raid sirens, ear-splitting explosions, screams of terror, clanging fire engines and urgent police cars. There was no possibility of military service: Evans was emphatically rejected on health grounds.

His life settled into a shiftless pattern. He went from one

menial job to another, unable to take on work that required a reasonable standard of education. With a little money and freedom to move about, he discovered the attraction of drink. It gave him solace, fired his imagination and gained him an audience for absurd claims of having rich relatives and aristocratic connections. His mother was used to his lies and would challenge him if they became too ridiculous. Evans was less worried about being caught out than of having his fibs reported to his elder sister, whom he idolized. 'Don't tell Eileen, Mam,' was a familiar refrain in the house.

There were short but recurring bouts of unemployment. During some of these, Evans would simply disappear and stay away from home for a couple of days. When his mother asked him where he had been, he would give vague excuses or say that he could not remember. Had he been recovering from a heavy drinking session? Spending time with a girlfriend or a prostitute? Sleeping overnight in an underground station during an air raid? Or was a young man whose life had hitherto been under the strict control of parents, teachers and medical staff simply asserting his independence?

Whatever the answer, it was a worrying development for his mother.

In 1946, she was able to keep a closer eye on him because they worked together in the same toy factory. That year the family moved to St Mark's Road. Now 22, Evans was still living at home, but spending a lot of his leisure time at one or other of his favourite pubs. The Kensington Palace Hotel (he called it KPH) and the Elgin were both in Ladbroke Grove, and the little Welshman was a familiar figure in both places. Egged on by his drinking companions, he would embark on flights of fancy. Among his other extravagant boasts was the claim that his father was an Italian count and his brother owned a fleet of expensive limousines.

Like other young men in search of sexual experience, he had visited prostitutes. If he had conventional girlfriends, he was unable to hold on to them for long. His arrogance, loquaciousness and scrawny physique would have deterred most girls, and he was further handicapped by a lack of money and education. Yet he was clearly confident in the presence of women. He had a natural ebullience that must have interested some of them, and a capacity for concealing his low intelligence. He was streetwise and could be shrewd.

When he was later examined in prison, Evans's mental age was assessed as being somewhere between 10 and 11, his vocabulary that of a 14-year-old. But these things would not have been so obvious to people who met him socially and listened to his drunken perorations, because he could look and sound like someone of normal intelligence. Much has been made of his illiteracy by some commentators, yet one of the officers on duty in Evans's cell in the days before his execution remembers that the prisoner was always reading comics or glancing through magazines and books. Evans also had enough wit to pick up chess fairly quickly and played many games with the men guarding him.

Evans met his future wife on a blind date. Beryl Thorley was a small, extremely pretty, rather immature young woman of 18 (see plate 9) who worked on the switchboard at Grosvenor House in Mayfair. Evans had a friend who knew one of Beryl's colleagues so the men decided to invite both women out to the cinema. Evans was immediately attracted to Beryl and she was quite taken with him, clear proof of how cleverly he could hide his deficiencies. Those who later tried to portray Evans as a 'mental defective' forgot that Beryl came from a respectable family and worked in an upper-class area of London: she would hardly fall in love with a complete half-wit, to use the language of the time.

Beryl lived in Cambridge Gardens, a short stroll away from St Mark's Road. Evans was soon calling to take her out on her own; their romance swiftly blossomed and they were engaged within a few weeks. Excited by his good fortune, Evans took his fiancée around to see his mother every evening. Beryl's own mother had died and her father worked in Brighton, and Mrs Probert was drawn to the girl with the air of an orphan about her. The couple were married at the Kensington Register Office on 20 September 1947. Mrs Probert paid all the expenses and the newlyweds moved into St Mark's Road.

It was a full house. In addition to her husband and her two daughters, Mrs Probert had tenants in the two top rooms.

Evans and his wife therefore took the second-floor back bedroom. It was quite usual at the time for young couples with limited income to move in with one or other set of parents, but it did mean that they never had real privacy. From Beryl's point of view, Evans's family could not have been more welcoming. For a lusty young man with a lovely bride, however, the situation must have been inhibiting at times.

Everyone in the house was employed. Mr Probert was still working as a decorator while his wife and stepdaughters all worked at Osram's, the same factory where Ethel Christie had worked during the war. Evans was now a van driver for Lancaster Food Products, a job that took him to various parts of the country. He must somehow have been able to make out details of deliveries in order to hold down his job.

Evans was happy. Marriage gave him pleasure, companionship and identity. It ratified his manhood. Beryl, too, was ecstatic in the early months. She had acquired a husband she loved, a substitute mother and two doting sisters-in-law.

MOVING IN WITH THE CHRISTIES

Early in 1948, Beryl Evans became pregnant and the search for new accommodation began. When the Evanses took the flat at Rillington Place, they liked the Christies and viewed them as a harmless couple who belonged to another generation. Eileen, however, took against Christie from the start; like most women, she found him unprepossessing. As she helped her brother to decorate the flat, she saw a great deal of Christie and he did not improve on acquaintance. What disturbed her most was his habit of creeping silently around the house in plimsolls. Eileen felt sorry for Christie's wife, who seemed to be quietly terrified of him.

Once the decorating was finished, furniture was bought on a hire purchase agreement with Mrs Probert standing surety. Evans and his wife moved in and quickly settled. Though they lived in two small rooms, had no bathroom and were denied use of the garden, they were nevertheless fond of their flat. Offered a far better one, Beryl did not want to move. With all its short-comings, she liked living in Rillington Place and considered the Christies 'all right'. It was to prove a fatal misjudgement.

Geraldine Evans was born at Queen Charlotte's Hospital in October 1948, to the family's delight. Evans was thrilled to be a father and loved to show her off to others. His mother doted on her first grandchild, and Eileen and Maureen were affectionate aunts. The baby seemed to complete the marriage. Evans did not see a great deal of Geraldine: he left the house early in the morning and—if he was driving outside London—did not return until well into the evening, though he and Beryl would then spend time together with the baby. Every Wednesday they went to the cinema, leaving Geraldine with her grandmother and picking her up afterwards. Evans went off to a drinking session on Saturdays, and called on his mother every Sunday to do any chores she required.

Tensions soon began to develop at Rillington Place. The young and inexperienced Beryl was a poor housekeeper, seldom cleaning the flat and often leaving piles of unwashed crockery in the kitchen. She rarely made her husband a hot meal and sometimes left him to fend for himself. Mrs Probert and her daughters were dismayed to see the state of the flat and helped to clean it up. More worrying was the fact that the baby, though well-fed, was often dirty. Eileen began taking her around to St Mark's Road on a Saturday to bathe her and give her a fresh change of clothes.

Evans chided his wife about her failings. There were frequent rows, loud enough to be heard by neighbours and by the other tenants. Though both parents loved their child, Geraldine's demands for food and attention only contributed to a growing tension further exacerbated by financial worries. Evans's wage of £7 or so a week was not enough to cover the rent, the repayments on the furniture, visits to the cinema and pub, and the shopping. Many of the quarrels revolved around Beryl's inability to spend what little money they had wisely.

The rows sometimes resulted in violence. From their windows, neighbours saw the couple exchanging blows and often watched Evans storming out of the house. Beryl always fought back. When she threw a jar at her husband's head, Evans had to rush off to his mother to get the wound dressed.

Well aware of what was going on in the top-floor flat, the Christies did not feel that it was their place to interfere.

The arrival of Beryl's friend Lucy Endecott — a pretty blonde of 17 — lifted marital stress to a new level. When the two young women shared the only bed for the night, Evans was forced to sleep on the kitchen floor, which he found demeaning. He threatened to leave; meanwhile Beryl began to suspect that Evans and Lucy were 'carrying on'. The resulting arguments sometimes escalated into brawls. On one occasion, after Beryl took up a bread knife to defend herself, Evans told his wife 'I'll push you through the bloody window' (MEPO 3/3147). At a later date, Lucy ended up going off with Evans. As he left, Evans warned his wife that he was not coming back. But when he and Lucy became fully intimate, one night of him was all she could stand. Evans arrived home from work next day to find a note of rejection from her, which he had to get someone to read for him.

Hearing that he had been thrown out, Evans had another tantrum. Driven into Lucy Endecott's arms by lust, desperation and an urge to exact revenge on his wife, now he had been rejected and his escape hatch had closed. Frothing with anger, he told his friends that he would run Lucy over in his van. This wild threat was very much in character: he never really intended to kill Lucy any more than he intended to hurl Beryl from the window of the flat. When he had cooled down, he was able to see how much more his wife and child offered him than the troublesome blonde who had come between them. Swallowing his pride, Evans went home to Beryl and apologized to her. She accepted him back.

Against the evidence of their occasional fights must be set the testimony of friends and babysitters who found them a delightful couple, patently fond of each other. Everyone commented on the fact that Evans adored the baby and helped to feed her. When the couple did quarrel, they usually made up afterwards. But they were still both young. Because neither had the intelligence or the composure to deal calmly with problems that arose, they blamed each other for each crisis and a row flared up. It was the sort of thing that happened between many working-class couples in the area.

Beryl's unplanned second pregnancy changed everything. The prospect of having to care for another baby was daunting. She would have to give up her part-time job and would be stuck in the flat with two demanding babies; not yet 20, she felt that she would be trapped. In a panic, she started douching and syringing herself, but these measures proved futile. When she told Evans that she wanted an abortion, he was against the idea. His wife was determined and tried various pills, to no avail. Having resolved on an abortion, she told her sisters-in-law, Eileen and Maureen, and Joan Vincent, an old schoolfriend who had met up with her again at the post-natal clinic.

John Christie also came to hear of it. He had been watching Beryl ever since she had come to live in Rillington Place. He saw the attractive and highly desirable young woman daily; every time she came down or went up the bare wooden staircase, she passed between the Christies' bedroom and kitchen. Beryl would have presented a dramatic contrast to Ethel, a vivacious girl compared to a middle-aged frump. The man who had persuaded Muriel Eady that he could cure her catarrh felt that he could persuade the equally gullible and unguarded Beryl Evans that he could perform an abortion.

The first stage in his plans was convincing Evans, and this was easily done. Taking him into his flat, Christie claimed that he had once trained to be a doctor before having to abandon his studies. He showed Evans his first aid manuals and told him they were medical textbooks. The bogus doctor said that he had performed abortions before, though there was an element of risk in some cases, and assured Evans that he would be happy to help his friends out of their predicament. Only someone as ignorant and unsuspecting as Evans would have been taken in by these lies, but the conversation was repeated to Beryl and she agreed to entrust herself to the nice man downstairs.

Full details of what happened on Tuesday 8 November 1949 will never be known. Christie did not divulge them and his separate versions of events are full of contradictions and ambiguities. But there are substantive facts that accord with the second police statement made by Evans at Merthyr Tydfil police station on 30 November (MEPO 3/3147). On the morning of 8 November, Evans got up at 6 am with his wife and had a cup of tea and a smoke. Beryl told him to tell Christie on his way out that 'everything was all right'. Anticipating the message, Christie came out to meet Evans when he heard him descending the stairs. The van driver went off to work, leaving the coast clear.

Around lunchtime, Christie crept upstairs in his plimsolls to find Beryl waiting nervously for him in the kitchen, wearing a spotted cotton blouse, a light blue woollen jacket and a black skirt. She brought a quilt from the front room and laid it down in front of the grate. Christie could not remember if the fire was lit; extraneous detail was of no interest to him. His mind was fixed on only one thing. Besides, he was already sexually aroused. Still fully dressed, Beryl lay obediently on the quilt; the likelihood is that she had already removed her knickers.

Christie had come prepared. He had brought a tube which he attached to the gas point, explaining that a sniff or two would help to ease the pain of the abortion. Now he had before him what he had fantasized about—a lovely young woman at his mercy, her naked thighs spread invitingly apart. He made his move. Beryl reacted at once, throwing the tube aside and struggling madly, but she was no match for a man in the grip of sexual frenzy. Punching her hard in the face until she was semi-conscious, Christie took out what he later referred to as 'my strangling rope' and squeezed the life out of her. A third hapless victim had been added to his tally.

CHAPTER TWO

Evans Stands Accused

===

Christie was denied the opportunity to gloat over the corpse of Beryl Evans. He heard footsteps ascending the staircase: it must have been a heart-stopping moment. Could it be his wife? Or one of the workmen who were in the house, carrying out repairs on the ground floor? Worst of all, could it be Evans, returning home unexpectedly? In fact, it was Joan Vincent, who had become a regular visitor to Rillington Place.

What Joan found unusual this time was that the front door had been left open for the workmen to come and go. She let herself in and went upstairs. Another surprise awaited her. The Evanses' kitchen door, customarily left open, was firmly shut. Knocking, she called out 'Beryl, it's me!' but there was no reply. When she tried the door, Mrs Vincent could only open it a matter of inches because of resistance from the other side.

She was justifiably upset. 'If you don't want to see me,' she said, 'you've only got to say so' (Ludovic Kennedy, *10 Rillington Place*). Assuming that Beryl had deliberately kept her out, she left. Ethel Christie, whom she met at the bottom of the stairs, told her that she did not know if Beryl had gone out.

Those who believe Timothy Evans murdered his wife argue that Christie would not have risked killing Beryl when other people were in the house. Kitchener, from the first-floor flat, was in hospital, but Ethel was still there and so were Willis and Jones, the two workmen who had been putting a new roof on the wash-house and lavatory. As the front door was ajar, there was always a chance of visitors letting themselves in. Christie took that chance. Ruthless and single-minded, he was so caught up in his exhilaration that he defied the risks. The blatancy of the crime was very much in character. This, after all, was a man who, having found that Muriel Eady's thigh bone had worked its way up through the soil, used it to prop up the garden fence.

Evans, meanwhile, was at work. He had strong reservations about the abortion, but was also aware of the practical advantages. Another child would place additional strain on the couple's already stretched finances. Geraldine would no longer be the centre of attention, and would resent that. He decided to let the abortion go ahead, reassured that it would be carried out on the premises by a man, as he thought, with sound medical knowledge — though he was alarmed by Christie's warning that one in every ten operations resulted in death.

When he arrived home that evening, Evans was met by Christie, who followed him upstairs. They entered the kitchen of the top flat and Evans lit the gaslight. 'It's bad news,' said Christie. 'It didn't work.' Evans reeled from the hammer blow.

In his second statement, made at Merthyr Tydfil police station
on 30 November 1949, he took up the story:

> I asked him where she was. He said, 'Laying on the bed in the
> bedroom.' Then I asked him where was the baby. So he said, 'The
> baby's in the cot.' So I went into the bedroom, I lit the gas then I
> saw the curtains had been drawn. I looked at my wife and saw that
> she was covered over with an eiderdown. I pulled the eiderdown
> back to have a look at her. (Evans quotes from MEPO 3/3147)

Christie had not only closed the curtains against the prying
eyes of neighbours, he had adjusted Beryl's collar to hide the
marks of strangulation on her neck. Evans was devastated:

> I could see that she was dead and that she had been bleeding
> from the mouth and the nose and that she had been bleeding
> from the bottom part… Christie was in the kitchen. I went
> over and picked up my baby. I wrapped the baby in a blanket
> and took her in the kitchen. Mr. Christie had lit the fire in the
> kitchen. He said, 'I'll speak to you after you feed the baby.'
> So I made the baby some tea and boiled an egg for her, then I
> changed the baby and put her to sit in front of the fire. Then
> I asked him how long my wife had been dead. He said, 'Since
> about three o'clock.' Then he told me my wife's stomach had
> been septic-poisoned.

Evans was too ignorant of medical matters to challenge Christie.
'He then told me to stop in the kitchen and closed the door and
went out. He came back about a quarter of an hour later and told

me that he had forced the door of Mr Kitchener's flat and had put my wife's body in there.' In fact, Christie needed Evans's help to carry the body downstairs. 'I asked him what he intended to do and he said, "I'll dispose of it down one of the drains." He then said, "You'd better go to bed and leave the rest to me." ' Christie had established control.

Evans's first concern had been for Geraldine. He wanted to take her to his mother, but Christie dissuaded him, saying that it would arouse suspicion. Tellingly, on one important point, Christie's later confession and Evans's second statement made in Merthyr Tydfil agree: Evans did not realize that his wife had been strangled. He believed that she had died as a result of the abortion. As Christie had carried out this illegal operation, he would be the one tried for manslaughter, but he was quick to point out that Evans would also be arrested on a charge of being an accessory before the fact. Beryl's death had to be concealed and the baby taken care of in some way.

Next morning, Christie told Evans that he knew a couple in East Acton who would look after Geraldine. The idea of losing his child to foster parents must have shaken Evans, but he could never look after her on his own. When he arrived home from work that evening, Evans fed Geraldine and played with her in front of the fire—hardly the action of a man who would later strangle her. Christie came up to tell him that the couple from East Acton would collect the baby on the following morning and that her clothes needed to be packed. If anyone asked where his wife and child were, Evans was to say that they had gone away on holiday. That was what Evans's mother was told when her son next called on her. Hearing that Beryl had taken the baby to visit her father, Mr Thorley, in Brighton, Mrs Probert responded tartly: 'He's bloody generous all of a sudden, isn't he?' When asked that same evening by Ethel Christie where his wife and child were, Evans replied that they had gone to Bristol. The change of destination may be put down to the fact that, after leaving St Mark's Road, Evans had called in at the Kensington Park Hotel for a drink or two.

DEATH OF AN INFANT

On the next day, Thursday 10 November, Evans got up early, fed and dressed Geraldine, then left her in her cot. On his way out, he handed over a suitcase of the baby's clothes to Christie, who told him that the couple would be taking the baby away that morning. In fact, the only people who came were the workmen plastering the wash-house. As they worked, they were unaware that Christie had slipped upstairs to strangle Geraldine Evans with a tie, which he left around the child's neck. In all probability, he concealed her with her mother in Kitchener's flat. He must have been aware that if the bodies of Beryl and her daughter were discovered, their deaths could be blamed on Evans: Christie later boasted to a prison psychiatrist that 'I could make Evans do or say anything I wanted' (CAB 143/18).

We know exactly how Christie behaved in the wake of a murder because he already had two victims to his name before he killed Beryl. He remained cool, watchful and manipulative. Given what we know of Evans's character, he would not have reacted in the same way. Had he really strangled his wife, he would have been more likely to bolt in fear, and if caught by the police, would have had no reason to accuse Christie of being the killer at that time: there was nothing to connect Christie with the crime except that he had been alone with Beryl—ostensibly performing an abortion—at the time of her death.

Joan Vincent now re-enters the story. When she called at the house to see Beryl and tax her about what had happened on her last visit, she once more found the front door open because the workmen were still there. Before she could go upstairs, however, she was accosted by Christie, who told her that mother and baby had gone away to Bristol. It was troubling news; Mrs Vincent could not believe that her friend would have left London without telling her.

Over Christie's shoulder, she could see into his sitting room and noticed Geraldine's pram and high chair. Christie explained that he was looking after them until they could be sent on. Mrs Vincent pressed for more detail, but Christie was evasive. Having always been polite before, he suddenly became abrupt, telling her that it would be much better if she did not come to the house any more, because her clothes were so much better than Beryl's that it made her jealous.

It was a bad day for Evans. Having lost a wife and (unbeknown to him) a daughter, he now lost his job as well. His employers had had enough of his laziness, lies and repeated requests for advance payment of his wages. When he asked for money to send on to Beryl in Brighton—he had diverted her from Bristol this time—he was given the sack. Evans returned to Rillington Place after the workmen had finished for the day: he was joined in his kitchen by Christie and told that the couple from East Acton had taken the baby away. Christie said that he would take the pram, high chair and other items to his friends later that week. When he heard that Evans had been dismissed from his job, Christie saw the ideal way to get rid of him.

If Evans remained in Rillington Place, he would attract visits from his mother and sisters who would press for details of Beryl's whereabouts. More worrying for Christie was the possibility that Evans might pop into Kitchener's flat to take a final look at his wife, only to find Geraldine there as well. It was essential to get Evans out of London altogether. As he had no job, the Welshman had no reason to stay in the house. The ever persuasive Christie advised him to sell his furniture and leave, and on the next day, Friday 11 November, Evans sold his furniture to Robert Hookway for £40 even though it had not been fully paid for.

Two events of significance happened that day. First, Willis and Jones completed their work and collected their tools from the wash-house, leaving it swept clean. For part of the day they had worked with carpenter Robert Anderson, who had pulled up rotten floorboards in the ground-floor passage. And second, Evans, at Christie's instigation, called on Joan Vincent. He and Mrs Vincent disliked each other, so it was an odd thing for Evans to do. Equally odd in her eyes was the fact that he was wearing a smart new camel-hair overcoat. She wondered how a man always in debt could afford £14—he told her the price—when his weekly wage was half that amount. Evans did as he had been bidden by Christie, explaining that Beryl had gone away with the baby and that she would be writing to her friend. But Mrs Vincent treated anything Evans said with caution.

Evans drifted through the next few days at the pictures, the pub and in bed, and arranged for a rag dealer to collect later from Rillington Place. Getting up at around 6 am on Monday, he tore up all his wife's clothing as well as cutting up the eiderdown and blanket. When the rag merchant called, he took away two full sacks. Hookway arrived that afternoon to collect the furniture. Evans recalled:

> The only thing left in the house then was vases, a clock, some dishes, saucepans and a bucket and the case with the baby's clothes, her pram and small chair. Christie had all that stuff. He asked me where I was going to go. I told him I don't know. Then I got my case. I took it up to Paddington, left it in the luggage department until half-past twelve that evening.

It was not the hasty departure of a killer trying to outrun the law, but a leisured withdrawal from a city that held too many sad memories. Evans went to the cinema before paying a last visit to one of his favourite pubs. After midnight, Evans collected his case and caught the train to Cardiff, where he changed to a local train that took him to Merthyr Vale, arriving well before 7 am.

His uncle and aunt were very surprised to see him at such an hour. Evans told them that he and his boss were touring the West Country with a view to opening new branches there, and that their car had broken down in Cardiff. He repeated the lie that Beryl and the baby had gone to Brighton. Evans claimed that it would take days to repair the car, and as they were fond of him, they were happy to have him stay there. After his uncle had gone off to work, his aunt made Evans a hearty breakfast and listened to all the news from London. Arriving in his smart new coat and with his hair slicked neatly down, he must have cut quite a figure: no longer the sickly boy who had been an outsider but a Welsh exile who had made good in London.

Evans went back to Cardiff the next day to collect the luggage he had left there, returning with a new white shirt and a brightly coloured tie. As with the purchase of the new coat, these were items intended to cheer him up. Evans had money in his pocket, but it did not stay there. He enjoyed the rare pleasure of spending freely with no thought of a future source of income.

He stayed at 93 Mount Pleasant for six days. On a couple of occasions, he went to the local pub with his uncle and bragged about metropolitan life. The Lynches would later recall how fondly and frequently their nephew talked about Geraldine.

There was a photograph of her on the wall and Evans was caught talking to it more than once, his eyes alight and a smile on his face. Clearly believing that the baby was still alive, he bought Geraldine a teddy bear from Woolworth's in Merthyr Tydfil.

At one point, he was seen examining a wedding ring. Asked by his uncle if it was Beryl's, Evans said he had simply picked it up somewhere. To get rid of an object that aroused disturbing memories, he later sold it in Merthyr Tydfil for a few shillings.

The stay in Wales must have relieved some of his tension, but Evans realized that he could not remain there for ever. His daughter's safety weighed on his mind. Evans was a practised liar, but even he would not have maintained the pretence that Geraldine was still alive unless he truly believed that she was. Had he killed the child himself, it seems unlikely that he would have gone to members of his family who would be sure to ask after her. 'Just wait till you see her, Auntie Vi. She's a smasher,' was only one of many affectionate things he said of her.

Concern for Geraldine eventually sent him back to London. Christie was alarmed to see him turn up on the doorstep, and when Evans asked to see his daughter told him that she needed two or three weeks to settle in with her foster parents. Wanting Evans out of the way, Christie did not invite him in. Instead, he claimed to be on his way to the doctor, and the two men caught the same bus—but Dr Odess had no record of a visit from Christie that day: Christie had lied to divert Evans.

Only partially satisfied, Evans returned to Wales. When asked about his wife and child, he said that Beryl had walked out on him and left the baby in her cot. He then made the extraordinary claim that people in Newport were looking after Geraldine for him. The Lynches were perplexed, and something else worried them: Evans had told them that he went to London to collect his wages, yet when he got back, he borrowed money from his uncle.

On Monday 28 November, Mrs Probert received a letter from Mrs Lynch telling her that her son had been in Wales for the last fortnight. She knew that Beryl and Geraldine had not gone to Brighton because her daughters had telegraphed Beryl's father. When Eileen had called at Rillington Place for information, Ethel Christie had told her that Beryl and the baby had left on Tuesday 8 November. On the day that Evans's mother got the letter, Maureen paid a visit to the house. Ethel Christie repeated her claim that Beryl and the baby had left on 8 November, saying goodbye and promising to write.

The conversation was interrupted by Christie. Usually placid, he was now in a temper. He told Maureen that Beryl had gone to Brighton and Evans to Bristol, adding that Evans had sold all the furniture. Maureen asked to see the flat, but Christie refused to let her in; he asserted that Beryl had walked out on Tuesday 8 November without saying a word to them. 'Well, one of you is telling lies,' said Maureen, 'because Mrs Christie just said Beryl said goodbye and that she would write' (Kennedy, *10 Rillington Place*). Before Ethel could speak, Christie told her to shut her mouth. He then derided Evans, saying he had marked him down as a bad lot when he was in the CID at Harrow Road.

Maureen defended Evans hotly. 'You're a bloody liar as my brother was in and out of hospitals and sanatoriums before we moved here.' She told him that if they hadn't heard of Beryl or Tim by Friday, she would ask her mother to go to the police. According to Maureen, this threat made Christie so angry that he almost struck her, 'saying he knew more about it than I thought he did. He also said that Tim wouldn't thank me if I brought the police into it.'

Bewildered and angry, Mrs Probert wrote to her sister-in-law.

> Well Vi I don't know what lies Tim have told you down there, I know nothing about him as I have not seen him for 3 weeks and I have not seen Beryl or the baby for a month... I done my best for him and Beryl, what thanks did I get, his name stinks up here, everywhere I go people asking for him for money he owes them, I am ashamed to say he is my son... (HO 45/25652)

Mrs Probert's bitterness is understandable. She had not only been left in the dark about the whereabouts of her son, her daughter-in-law and granddaughter, she had been forced to pay the money outstanding on the furniture from the flat. Maureen also sent a letter to Mount Pleasant, threatening to kill her brother for the worry he had caused their mother. When the Lynches questioned him, Evans could not talk his way out of the situation.

1 View of Rillington Place in Notting Hill, West London, around the time of Christie's crimes. On nearby streets John Christie lingered, looking for prostitutes and potential victims.

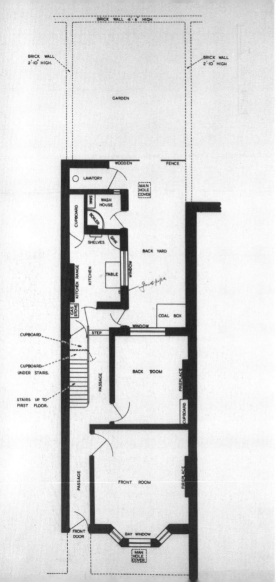

2 Plan of the ground floor of 10 Rillington Place used in the Christie trial. At various times bodies were found in the wash-house, kitchen, front room and garden. (HO 291/228)

METROPOLITAN POLICE TELEGRAM.

30-11-49

TO CH/SUPT FH FROM IR.

THE FOLLOWING TELEPHONE MESSAGE RECEIVED FROM POLICE, MERTHYR-TYDFIL (TELE. 541). BEGINS:-

'A MAN NAMED TIMOTHY JOHN EVANS HAS COME TO THIS STATION THIS AFTERNOON AND STATED THAT ON 8-11-49 AT 10, RILLINGTON PLACE, W.11., HIS WIFE HAD A MISCARRIAGE AT THAT ADDRESS, AFTER WHICH SHE APPARENTLY DRANK SOME LIQUID WHICH HE OBTAINED FROM A LORRY DRIVER SOME TIME PREVIOUS AT A CAFE BETWEEN CHELMSFORD AND IPSWICH. DURING THE NIGHT OF 9-11-49 BETWEEN 1AM AND 2.AM HE DISPOSED OF HIS WIFES BODY DOWN A MANHOLE OR DRAIN OUTSIDE THAT ADDRESS. HE HANDED HIS 14 MONTH OLD CHILD TO A MAN NAMED REGINALD CHRISTIE AT THE SAME ADDRESS WHO STATED HE COULD HAVE THE CHILD TAKEN CARE OF. HE ALSO SOLD THE FURNITURE AND LEFT THE ADDRESS. WILL YOU PLEASE CAUSE ENQUIRIES TO BE MADE. A WRITTEN STATEMENT HAS BEEN TAKEN FROM EVANS. ENDS.

FORWARDED FOR NECESSARY ACTION ON DIRECTIONS OF CH/SUPT C-1.

T. OF O. 6-8 PM.

FORWARDED:- 6-46 PM.

ACTION COPIES:- C-1(10)

3 *Above*: The Metropolitan Police telegram reporting Timothy Evans's surrender to the Welsh police on 30 November 1949—at that time Evans did not seem to know the true location of Beryl's corpse. (MEPO 3/3147)

4 *Right*: The press photograph of Evans under police escort at Paddington station after travelling from Wales to London for questioning.

Continuation of Statement of   Timothy John EVANS.

of the fire/

with my baby. I made the baby a feed about 9.30 p.m. I fed her
then I changed her, then I put her to bed. I come back into
the kitchen sat by the fire until about twelve o'clock, then went
to bed. I got up at 6 a.m. next day, lit the gas put the kettle
on, made the baby a feed and fed it. I then changed her and
dressed her. I then poured myself out a cup of tea I had already
made. I drank half and the baby drank the other half. I then
put the baby back into the cot, wrapped her up well and went to
work. I done my day's work and then had an argument with the
Guvnor then I left the job. He give me my wages before I went
home. He asked me what I wanted my wages for. I told him I
wanted to post some money off to my wife first thing in the
morning. He asked where my wife was and I told him she had gone
to Bristol on a holiday. He said, "How do you intend to send
the money to her" and I said, "In a registered envelope". He
paid me the money so he said, "You can call over tomorrow morning
for your cards". I then went home, picked up my baby from her
cot in the bedroom, picked up my tie and strangled her with it.
I then put the baby back in the cot and sat down in the kitchen
and waited for Christies downstairs to go to bed. At about
twelve o'clock that night I took the baby downstairs to the
washhouse and hid her body behind some wood. I then locked the
washhouse door behind me and came in closing the back door behind
me. I then slipped back upstairs and laid on the bed all night,
fully clothed. I got up the following morning, washed, shaved
and changed, and went up to see a man in Portabella Road about
selling my furniture. I don't know his name. During the same /
afternoon

Signature..

Signature witnessed by..

No. 993

Continuation of Statement of *John Reginald Halliday Christie*

but it was impossible I couldn't bend over. I think thats when I strangled her. I think it was with a stocking I found in the room. The gas wasn't on very long. Not much over a minute I think. Perhaps one or two minutes. I then left her where she was and went downstairs. I think my wife was downstairs. She didn't know anything about it. Evans came home in the evening about six o'clock. It was dark. When I heard him come in, I went to my kitchen door and called him. I spoke to him in the passage and told him that his wife had committed suicide, that she had gassed herself. I went upstairs with him. We went into the kitchen and Evans touched his wife's hand, then picked her up and carried her into the bedroom and put her on the bed. It was dark, there were no lights on in the kitchen or the bedroom. I feel certain it was a stocking I strangled her with. I didn't tie it round the neck. I just

Signature *J R Christie*

Signature witnessed by

Use both sides if necessary. (If this is done, both sides of the form must be signed and witnessed).

6 *Left*: John Christie's prison confession on 8 June 1953 to the murder of Beryl Evans. The previous page admits that he tried to have intercourse with her. (MEPO 2/9535)

7 *Below*: The wash-house at Rillington Place where the bodies of Beryl and Geraldine Evans were found. (CRIM 1/2035)

5 *Left*: Evans's Notting Hill statement on 2 December 1949 confessing to the murder of his wife after being confronted with her and Geraldine's clothing. (MEPO 3/3147)

Rex v Evans

heard at the Old Bailey on Friday the 13th of Jan, 1950

THIS is a report of the Old Bailey trial of Timothy John Evans, who was sentenced to death on Friday the 13th of January 1950, for the murder of his 14 - month - old daughter, Geraldine:

The prosecution said that the strangled bodies of Evans's 20-year-old wife, Beryl Susanna, and his daughter were found by the police on December 2, 1949, wrapped up in parcels in a wash-house at his home at 10, Rillington-place, Notting Hill.

Evans, who said he could not read or write, repeated the oath after the court usher when he went into the witness-box.

No idea

He denied in evidence being responsible for the death of either his wife or child.

He alleged that John Reginald Halliday Christie, who lived in another flat in the house, said he was going to treat his wife to end her pregnancy. When Evans returned from work on November 8 Christie told him he had some bad news—Mrs. Evans was dead.

While Evans was feeding the baby he heard Christie coughing and blowing on the stairs.

On going out, Evans said he saw him trying to get the body of Mrs. Evans down the stairs.

He added: "I helped Christie to carry my wife's body to an empty flat and never saw her again."

He also said Christie told him he would make arrangements for friends to look after the baby.

On November 10, on returning home from work, Evans said he was informed that the child had been collected by those friends.

Later, said Evans, he went to stay with relatives in Wales, and he told them his wife and the baby were staying with other relatives.

All untrue

Evans also said that he had no idea his daughter had been strangled until told by the police.

He was asked why he told the police at Merthyr Tydfil—where he gave himself up—that he had disposed of his wife's body in a drain. He said this was not true, but was said to "protect" Christie.

Replying to Mr. Christmas Humphreys (prosecuting) Evans admitted he made five different statements confessing to the murder of his wife and child. But he declared they were all untrue.

Evidence was called of statements alleged to have been made by Evans telling of repeated nagging by his wife which ended in his strangling her.

The prosecution also alleged that Evans sold his wife's wedding ring for six shillings to a South Wales jeweller, and later disposed of her furniture.

Christie, in the witness-box, denied any knowledge of the death of either Evans's wife or child. He also denied he had disposed of their bodies.

'A lie'

Mr. Malcolm Morris (defending): I have to suggest to you that you are responsible for the death of Mrs. Evans and the little girl or if that isn't so, at least you know much more about these deaths than you have said?

Christie: That is a lie.

He also denied that, after learning Mrs. Evans was pregnant he told her husband that he could relieve her of her condition without any risk. He said he advised her not to take the pills she was using.

Medical evidence was given which established that Mrs. Evans died from strangulation, and there was no sign of interference to end her pregnancy.

Summing up, Mr. Justice Lewis

THE EVANS BABY —GERALDINE.

Turn to Page 2, Col. 5

NG CHRISTIE STORY—PAGE THREE

8 *Left*: *Daily Mail* report on the Evans trial highlighting the conflicting accounts of Evans and Christie. (MEPO 2/9535)

9 *Below*: Murder victim Beryl Evans.

10 *Right*: Christie's description of how he murdered his wife, from his first statement on 31 March 1953. (MEPO 2/9535)

at about 8.15 and I think it was
by my wife moving about in bed.
I sat up and saw that she appeared
to be convulsive, her face was blue
and she was choking. I did what
I could to try and restore breathing
but it was hopeless. It appeared
too late to call for assistance.
That's when I couldn't bear to see
her, so I got a stocking and
tied it round her neck to put
her to sleep. Then I got out of
bed and saw a small bottle and
a cup half full of water on a
small table near the bed. I noticed
that the bottle contained two
Phenal Barbitone tablets and it
originally contained twenty-five.
I then knew that she must have
taken the remainder. I got them
from the Hospital because I
couldn't sleep. I left her in bed
for two or three days and didn't
know what to do. Then I remembered
some loose floor-boards in the
front room. I had to move a table
and some chairs to roll the lino
back about half way. Those

Signature *J.R. Christie*

Signature witnessed by

Use both sides if necessary. (If this is done, *both* sides of the form must be signed and witnessed).

M.P.-45530/200,000 Oct./1951 o25 (4)

9

11 *Above*: Ethel Christie in the garden of Rillington Place. (HO 291/228)

12 *Right*: Note written by Christie after Ethel's murder to her sister Lily Bartle, explaining that Ethel could not write her Christmas cards because of rheumatism. (HO 291/228)

EVANS'S SURRENDER

Conscience-stricken and yielding to pressure from his family, Evans went to Merthyr Tydfil police station on Wednesday 30 November.

Detective Constable Gwynfryn Evans was on duty. 'I want to give myself up,' said Evans. 'I have disposed of my wife.' When the detective asked him what he meant, Evans's reply was significant: 'I put her down the drain.' Warned to be careful what he was saying, Evans spoke firmly. 'I know what I'm saying. I can't sleep and I want to get it off my chest.'

Evans was taken to the CID in Merthyr Tydfil. After being cautioned again, he gave his first statement. The story was unbelievable. Evans claimed that his wife had become pregnant and wanted an abortion. Meeting a man in a café in East Anglia, Evans told him about the problem and the man gave him some pills to effect the abortion. When Beryl took them, they killed her. In the early hours of the morning, Evans claimed, he had carried his wife's body downstairs and pushed her head-first into the drain outside the house. Having found someone to look after his baby, he sold the furniture and went to Wales.

A call was immediately put through to Notting Hill (see plate 3). As a result, a police car was despatched to Rillington Place. There was a manhole outside Christie's front-room window but it took three policemen to lift it. The shaft was empty. Confronted with this information, Evans was mystified.

He had taken pains to keep Christie's name out of his statement because he believed that his friend had put Beryl down the drain. Hearing that the manhole cover was too heavy for one man to lift, he realized that Christie had lied to him. He no longer felt obliged to protect him.

Evans's second statement is probably as close to the truth as we are likely to get. He began not long after 9 pm and finished just before midnight. In total he had been at the police station for almost nine hours and his nerves must have been frayed. He talked about the failed abortion and Christie's promise to dispose of the body down the drain then hand over the baby to a couple in East Acton. There was no hint of murder having occurred. The only thing that Christie was accused of was carrying out an illegal abortion.

After a night at the police station, Evans was questioned again by Detective Constable Gwynfryn Evans. It was the morning of 1 December 1949. The detective asked him when he had last seen his wife's body. 'Just before Christie took it to Kitchener's flat,' replied Evans. 'Did you help Christie to carry it down?' asked the detective. Evans replied:

> Well, what happened was that Christie told me to stay in the kitchen, I listened and heard him puffing and blowing, and I saw him halfway down the stairs between my place and Kitchener's. The body of my wife was on the stairs. I said to Christie 'What's up?' and he said, 'I can't move her any further. Come and give me a hand.' I went down… That's the truth and that's the last time I saw her body.

The police in Notting Hill, meanwhile, had not been idle. When Evans's second statement had been phoned through to them, they called on Mrs Probert after midnight to ask where Beryl and the baby were. She repeated what she had been told. She was baffled by a message sent by her son, asking her to contact Christie in order to find out the address of the couple in East Acton who had adopted Geraldine. Mrs Probert readily admitted to the police that her son was a compulsive liar.

Later that day, the police searched 10 Rillington Place, although they did not really know what they were looking for. Failing to notice the human bone holding up the fence, they went upstairs to the top flat. Here they found a stolen briefcase and newspaper cuttings about the Stanley Setty torso murder, a crime for which Donald Hume was later convicted as an accessory. Why Evans, an illiterate man, should keep the cuttings is puzzling; it is more likely that Christie, who did cut items from newspapers, put them there to incriminate Evans. Ironically, the wash-house was not searched by the police. With two corpses under their noses and two more buried in the garden, all they found were the briefcase and newspaper clippings.

It was time to bring Evans to London for further questioning. Detective Inspector Black and Detective Sergeant Corfield were sent to Wales to arrest him on a charge of stealing the briefcase. Christie, meanwhile, was summoned to Notting Hill police station. Familiar with police routine and jargon, he was completely at ease even though he was there overnight for six hours. Hearing of Evans's accusations, he dismissed them as absurd. 'At no time have I assisted or attempted to abort Mrs Evans or any other women... I cannot understand why Evans should make such accusations against me, as I've really been very good to him in a lot of ways.'

Christie carefully laid down the poison. Evans and his wife, he said, were always arguing; she was afraid that Evans would kill her one day and had told Ethel Christie so. Christie said that he knew about Beryl's attempts to abort herself by syringing and douching. 'I said to her, in my wife's presence, that she was looking a physical wreck and advised her to stop it. We warned her of the consequences...' The constant use of his wife's name was deliberate. Christie knew that Ethel would be interviewed independently by the police and he had schooled her in what to say. A united front was presented. A respectable middle-aged married couple would always inspire more trust than a loud-mouthed, hot-headed young Welshman.

Christie had even taken the precaution of invalidating any evidence that Joan Vincent might give about her visit to the house on the day of the murder. According to Ethel, 'Mrs Evans did mention that a friend of hers called Joan had made trouble between her and her husband and that Joan was coming round that morning and that she (Mrs Evans) did not want to see her... Mrs Evans locked herself in the kitchen and refused to see her.' Buttressed by her husband's evidence, the word of Ethel Christie outweighed that of a young woman like Joan Vincent.

Having established that Beryl and the baby were neither in Brighton nor Bristol, the police conducted another search at the house. When they entered the wash-house, it was so dark that they needed a torch. A stack of wood was propped up against the sink. One of the officers felt something behind the wood. It was a package, wrapped in a green tablecloth and tied with a sash cord.

Ethel Christie was asked if she knew what it was, but even though she touched the package, she could not identify it. It was lifted outside the wash-house and the cord was loosened. Beryl Evans's feet flopped into view. And a second horror greeted the policemen. Hidden under more wood behind the door was the body of Geraldine, the tie that had strangled her still around her neck. With dramatic speed, the case had moved on to a new level.

While Christie had been relaxed in a police station, Evans had been unnerved. Held in custody and questioned without a solicitor present, he felt physically intimidated. Two London detectives then arrived to charge him with larceny and take him back to the capital. They spoke very little to him on the journey, and he must have been terrified. Innocent of stealing the briefcase and having no criminal record, he was nevertheless treated like a felon. When they arrived at Paddington station, a press photographer took a picture of him, a tiny, frightened, exhausted, white-faced man in the grip of detectives who towered over him (see plate 4).

At Notting Hill police station, Evans was shown two piles of clothing. Beryl's pile contained the blanket, tablecloth and sash cord. On Geraldine's pile was the tie used to strangle her. Evans stared at them in horror. Detective Chief Inspector Jennings told him that the bodies of his wife and child had been found behind wood in the wash-house at 10 Rillington Place. Death in both cases was by strangulation with a ligature. While Evans was struggling to cope with the enormity of it all, the detective went on. 'I have reason to believe that you were responsible for their deaths.' Stunned, Evans could manage only one word — 'Yes.'

Throughout the night of 2 and 3 December, Evans was interrogated by Jennings and Detective Inspector Black. Tired, gaunt and locked in the menacing environment of a police station, the prisoner gave two statements (see plate 5). They are worth comparing with those made in Merthyr Tydfil where Evans's authentic voice can be heard. At Notting Hill, there is a suggestion of ventriloquism. The statements contain words and phrases that an uneducated man would never use. Jennings took down the first confession in his notebook:

> She was incurring one debt after another and I could not stand it any longer, so I strangled her with a piece of rope and took her down to the flat below the same night whilst the old man was in hospital. I waited till the Christies had gone to bed, then I took her to the wash-house after midnight. This was on Tuesday 8th November. On Thursday evening after I came home from work I strangled the baby in the bedroom with my tie and later that night I took her down to the wash-house after the Christies had gone to bed.

The statement is palpably false. On Tuesday 8 November and for the next two and a half days, the workmen were in and out of the wash-house all the time. It would have been impossible to conceal two bodies from them in such a small area. The wood behind which Beryl was hidden had been taken up from the ground-floor passage by the carpenter on Friday 11 November and given to Christie on Monday 14 November. If the police had paid heed to this chronology, they could not possibly have charged Evans.

Evans's second, much longer statement must have taken hours to draw out of him. He claimed that it was five in the morning when they finished, though the statement is not timed. Giving far more detail, Evans admitted having violent rows with his wife over the fact that she was getting them into debt. Blows were exchanged on the evening of Tuesday 8 November. 'In a fit of temper I grabbed a piece of rope from the chair which I had brought home off my van and strangled her with it.' Why would he bring rope up to the flat and why leave it conveniently over the chair? It does not ring true, and yet this was what he admitted.

Evans also claimed that he had locked the dead bodies in the wash-house when, in fact, it was impossible to lock it. Never having been into the place, he did not realize this. The second statement repeated the patent lie that Beryl's corpse had been placed there on the Tuesday behind wood that was not even taken up until Friday. It was almost as if Evans had given up in despair, agreeing to everything that was put to him because he could see no way out. The police believed they had corroboration. Both Christie and Ethel had sworn that they had been awakened by a thud above their heads around midnight on 8 November. If they heard a noise from Kitchener's flat, it is surprising they did not hear other sounds if Evans really did carry the body of his wife down the uncarpeted stairs past their flat.

Preparing the case for the prosecution, the police interviewed the Christies and Joan Vincent. Ethel Christie placed Mrs Vincent's visit on Monday 7 November, the day before Beryl was killed, but she was either mistaken or deliberately misleading. Bad weather had kept the workmen away from the house on the Monday so the front door would not have been left open for a visitor to walk in. The police, however, convinced Mrs Vincent that she must have called on the Monday.

The workmen needed more persuasion. If their time sheets were correct and their comments about the state of the washhouse were true, the prosecution would be in severe difficulty. Nobody had seen Beryl Evans alive after Tuesday 8 November yet two of the workmen deposed that nothing was hidden under a sink while they were working there. Willis, Jones and their boss were hauled along to the police station and kept there for hours, during which they were persuaded that there *might* have been timber in front of the sink that went unnoticed. No statement was taken from Anderson, the carpenter who had worked at the house on the Friday and following Monday. Christie never explained why the timber given him for firewood had lain unused in the wash-house for two and a half weeks during a cold November.

On remand in Brixton prison, Evans was in the hospital ward, able to relax for the first time in weeks. Popular with staff and prisoners, he seems to have been in a cheerful mood. 'There are eighteen of us in here,' he said, 'and we play dominoes and games of all kinds.' (Tennyson Jesse) By a bizarre coincidence, Donald Hume, held in connection with the Stanley Setty murder, was also in the ward. Evans was wary of him — 'you have to watch Hume' — a comment which undermines the notion that Evans killed his wife as a copycat crime.

Evans was not well served by his solicitors. Granted legal aid, he chose the firm of Messrs Freeborough, Slack and Co. Geoffrey Freeborough and his chief clerk, Baillie Saunders, a man in his eighties, were not sanguine. Although Evans was now pleading his innocence and accusing Christie of murder, the evidence against him was formidable. Saunders failed to do any of the things that would have aided Evans's defence, such as talking to the workmen from 10 Rillington Place, interviewing Joan Vincent and paying attention to the telling conversation between Christie and Evans's sister, Maureen, on 28 November. Had he investigated Christie's past, Saunders would have learned about his criminal record.

At the first hearing at the magistrates' court on 15 December, the Christies gave evidence. Coached by her husband in what to say, Ethel was under such strain that she broke down when she entered the witness box. Christie claimed that he was unwell and was allowed a seat when he gave evidence. At the second hearing a week later, Evans's statements and police evidence were given. The prisoner was remanded in custody for trial at the Central Criminal Court. Early in the New Year, Freeborough delivered his brief to Malcolm Morris, the barrister leading the defence.

On the morning of 11 January 1950, the case of Rex v Timothy John Evans opened at No. 1 Court at the Old Bailey. The judge was Mr Justice Lewis, an experienced but ailing man who died shortly after the trial. Leading the prosecution was Christmas Humphreys, taking his first case as Senior Treasury Counsel and eager to impress on his debut. He secured an advantage at the very start. Evans was charged with the murder of his daughter. He pleaded not guilty. Morris objected to the fact that the prosecution also intended to introduce evidence relating to Beryl's death. After sending out the jury, the judge listened to the objection, but ruled in favour of the prosecution. In effect, Evans would now be tried for two murders.

When the jury returned, Humphreys made his opening speech. 'The case for the Crown is that this man and his wife got on badly, that he got depressed because he lost his job, that he got more and more depressed and that then, as he himself said, he killed his wife and then killed his child.' Humphreys went on to describe Evans's movements from 8 November, detailing the lies he had told to explain the disappearance of his wife and child. The inconsistencies in his statements to the police were highlighted. Close attention was called to Evans's two confessions at Notting Hill.

Dr Teare was the first prosecution witness. In evidence regarding his post-mortem, he made no mention of the possibility of sexual penetration of Beryl Evans after death—which might have provided a motive for a killer other than Evans. He had examined the vagina with a microscope, but no swab had been taken.

John Christie was the Crown's chief witness and he gave a convincing performance. He talked about the constant marital disputes in the Evanses' flat, the threats of murder and the thud in the middle of the night. Questioned about Evans's accusations against him, Christie claimed that he was suffering from enteritis and fibrositis on Tuesday 8 November, making it impossible for him to move properly. He had spent part of the day in bed. References to his service in the First World War and to his work as a policeman during the Second World War crystallized in the minds of the jury the image of a decent, honourable man, an image they took home at the end of the first day.

Christie did not celebrate his success. He went straight off to the doctor's surgery, and Dr Odess noted that the patient was very depressed. It is hardly surprising: if he gave himself away in court, Christie's life would be in peril.

Next day, it was Morris's turn to cross-examine the witness. Asked if he knew a young couple who lived in East Acton, Christie was able to answer honestly that he did not because he had invented them for Evans's benefit. After early skirmishing, Morris tried to strike home. He said: 'Well, Mr Christie, I have got to suggest to you, and I do not want there to be any misapprehension about it, that you are responsible for the death of Mrs. Evans and the little girl; if that is not so, that you know very much more about the deaths than you have said.'

Christie's reply was firm. 'That is a lie.'

Morris managed to score a few points against Christie, but did not succeed in damaging his credibility as a witness. At the end of his cross-examination, he produced what he hoped would be a crucial blow: having heard about Christie's criminal record at the start of the trial, he now drew it to the court's attention in the hope that the jury would view the witness in a new light. But Humphreys countered by establishing that Christie's record had been unblemished for the past 17 years, and the jury seemed to feel that it was to Christie's credit that he was a reformed character living a blameless life.

When the defence opened its case, Evans was called by the clerk of the court. The prisoner was a pathetic figure, small, slight, lean and with a hunted look. Overwhelmed by the situation, he did his best to answer the questions truthfully. Morris first got him to deny any involvement in the murder of his wife and child then took him step by step through the events of Tuesday 8 November. What Evans said is substantially what appears in the second statement made in Merthyr Tydfil. Morris confirmed that Evans first heard about the murders when he met Jennings at Notting Hill police station.

'He told you that your wife and baby —'
    '— had been found dead, sir.'
    'Did he say where?'
    'Yes, sir. No 10 Rillington Place in the wash-house, and he
said he had good reason to believe I had something to do with it.'
    'Did he say how it appeared they died?'
    'Yes, sir, by strangulation.'
    'Did he say with what?'
    'Well, a rope, sir, my wife, and my daughter had been strangled
with a necktie.'
    'Was anything shown to you at the same time?'
    'Yes, sir, the clothing of my wife and daughter.'
    'Was there also a green tablecloth and a blanket?'
    'Yes, sir.'
    'And a length of rope?'
    'Yes, sir.'
    'I do not want to ask the same question twice, but before he
told you, had you any idea that anything had happened to your
daughter?'
    'No, sir. No idea at all.'
    'Did he tell you, when he said the bodies had been found in
the wash-house, whether they had been concealed or not?'
    'Yes, sir. He told me they had been concealed by timber.'

In short, every detail in Evans's first confession at Notting Hill
was given to him by the police. It was almost as if the statement
had been dictated. When asked why he had confessed, Evans

said that he was frightened of being beaten up by the police. He also recalled being very upset at the time: 'I had been believing my daughter was still alive.' When asked if he had anything left to live for when she was dead, he replied, 'No, sir.'

Cross-examination by Humphreys was fierce and unrelenting. Morris made some interventions to protect his client, but they did not save him. Put under great pressure, Evans was made to look foolish and dishonest. Confusing the exhibits, he answered questions about Exhibit 9 (his second statement at Notting Hill) in the belief that he was being asked about his first statement at Merthyr Tydfil. When pressed, Evans failed to suggest a motivation for Christie strangling his wife or his daughter, and Humphreys berated him for accusing 'a perfectly innocent man'.

Humphreys sat down: the case for the defence was over. As it was well into the afternoon, Morris assumed that by the time the closing speech for the prosecution had been made, it would be the end of court proceedings for the day. Relying on having several hours to marshal his defence, Morris was caught off guard when Humphreys spoke for less than ten minutes. Inadequately prepared, Morris tried to offer a cogent defence, but he was fighting a losing battle.

He rightly concentrated on the second Merthyr Tydfil statement as being the most accurate, refusing to accept that Evans could have made up so much detail. But to save his client, he had to discredit Christie, and acted on instructions to do so. 'Christie may be an abortionist,' he argued, 'and if that is so, something may have happened to Mrs Evans at Christie's hands on the afternoon of Tuesday 8 November, something perhaps which caused her to lapse into unconsciousness.' In the circumstances, he suggested, Christie might have been 'very frantic' and, knowing of her marital difficulties and of the way she had been spending money, he might have strangled her.

It was an unconvincing line of argument, weakened by Morris's obvious lack of enthusiasm for it. He was on surer ground when he pointed out that Evans had no police record. 'So what happens is that the one witness for the Prosecution who matters comes before you as someone who is not of good character and the man who is in the dock before you as a man who is.' But there was a note of apology at times that made the speech lack real conviction; where Humphreys had been terse, analytical and brilliant, Morris was tentative, telling the jury:

> So I ask you to think about it tomorrow…to bring every effort
> that you conceivably can to bear, every power that you have,
> and when you have done that, and have been as careful and as
> fair as I know you will be, Evans will be satisfied, and I, as his
> advocate, cannot ask for anything more.

Fearing the worst, Timothy Evans wilted in the dock.

CHAPTER THREE

Gruesome Discoveries

The fate of Timothy John Evans was decided on 13 January 1950. As Christie's fate also hung in the balance, he was in court to hear the summing-up by Mr Justice Lewis. The judge began by warning the jury that they must be satisfied beyond all reasonable doubt of Evans's guilt, and reminded them that their verdict would only relate to the murder of the child, although both murders had been considered by the court. He went carefully through the evidence, beginning with Christie's allegations and pointing out his physical problems on 8 November. 'He has told you, you know, he could not even stoop down to pick up anything off the floor. He was in great pain' (MEPO 3/3147).

If there was sympathy for Christie, there was none for Evans. The judge turned to Evans's first statement made in Merthyr Tydfil and heaped ridicule on the story of the man in the café and the bottle of abortion pills. Of the statement confessing to the crime made at Notting Hill, he said, 'He [Evans] gave as his reason for making the statement that he was heartbroken at hearing that his child was dead and had nothing left to live for, and so therefore he confessed to a crime he did not commit.'

When he added that the confession was also made to protect Christie—a mistaken assumption which ignored alternative explanations, such as Evans's fear and confusion—the judge was seriously misleading the jury. It was in his first statement at Merthyr Tydfil that Evans sought to shield Christie by keeping his name out of it. When he no longer felt the need to protect him, he described Christie's words and actions in the definitive second statement at Merthyr Tydfil.

The medical evidence was crucial. As long as Evans persisted with his claim about an attempted abortion, he was doomed, because the post-mortem showed that, in the judge's words, 'there was no mark of interference upon this woman'. Evans's claim was pitted against the expert opinion of Dr Teare.

The longer it went on, the more prejudiced became the judge's summing-up against Evans. During his defence, Malcolm Morris had drawn attention to the striking similarity between what Evans had said in the second Merthyr Tydfil statement and what he repeated in the witness box. Six weeks had passed since Evans had gone voluntarily to the police and he had had no opportunity to look at this statement in the interim. The judge discounted this.

Mr Justice Lewis exonerated Christie from lying by pointing out that the witness had acknowledged he knew about Beryl's pregnancy when he could easily have feigned ignorance. Everything turned on 'whether you accept Christie's evidence against this man or whether you accept this man against Christie'. He reminded the jury of Christie's war service and how he had been gassed and blinded and, referring to Christie's criminal past, emphasized that there had been 'no stain on his character whatsoever' in the last 17 years. The jury was asked to decide if such a man could really be an abortionist and a killer.

The judge was less flattering about Evans's character. 'The man has lied and lied and lied again. There is no doubt about it. He says it himself. He made three statements which are entirely untrue, and he has prevaricated all the way through the proceedings.' This was unfair. Anyone reading the transcript of the trial can see that Evans did not prevaricate: he stuck to what he believed was the truth. Rehearsing the discrepancies between the various statements, the judge repeated his mistaken assumption about the two confessions made at Notting Hill. 'Why did he go back and apparently in his third and fourth statements again try to protect Christie?'

By the end of his long, painstaking and biased summing-up, Mr Justice Lewis had left nobody in any doubt about whose word he believed. The verdict, however, lay in the hands of the jury, and they were directed to leave the court, taking with them copies of all four statements made by Evans. It took only 40 minutes for them to reach a decision: Timothy John Evans was found guilty of the murder of Geraldine Evans (see plate 8).

Asked if he had anything to say before judgement was passed, Evans replied in the negative. The judge donned the black cap and pronounced the death sentence. Alone in the large dock, Evans looked tiny, fragile and utterly friendless. Attention, however, had now shifted to Christie: when he realized that another man would be hanged for his crimes, he gave full vent to his feelings of relief and sobbed uncontrollably.

As the Christies left the court, they encountered Mrs Probert in the hallway. Close to hysteria, she pointed to Christie and yelled 'Murderer, murderer!' (Kennedy) Ethel Christie sprang to his defence: 'Don't you dare call my husband a murderer,' she retorted. 'He's a good man.'

The next day the Christies went off to stay in Sheffield. Evans, meanwhile, languished in Pentonville Prison. His appeal—on the grounds that evidence of his wife's death should not have been admitted during the trial—was dismissed on 20 February 1950. He swore to his mother and others that he was innocent, but did not seem to realize what would happen to him: he even talked about resuming his work as a driver. He ate and slept well, and officers on cell watch said that he spent his time reading and playing cards, and chatting about sport. He mentioned Beryl with respect, but never talked about Christie.

Timothy Evans was hanged on 9 March 1950. There was no public outcry: everyone apart from his family accepted his guilt. Meanwhile Christie's health had deteriorated. On returning from Sheffield, he went to see Dr Odess and broke down in tears; the doctor recommended a holiday. Christie was losing weight and unable to sleep. Because of disclosures in court about his criminal record, he lost his job at the Post Office

Savings Bank, which intensified an already deep depression. On the day after Evans was hanged, Christie again consulted Dr Odess who, unaware that Christie was now out of work, thought his condition serious enough to grant him a sick note for four weeks. It was a pity that Dr Odess's notes were not available during Evans's trial: they would have shown that Christie was not crippled by fibrositis, as he claimed, on 8 November 1949. It was days later that the ailment was diagnosed, after he had strained his back moving the dead body of Beryl Evans.

John Christie's medical history repays study. Throughout his life, he suffered from real or imaginary illnesses. Between 1937 and 1952, he made 173 visits to the surgery in Colville Square. There was a period during 1949 when he stayed away for seven months. The moment that he heard of Beryl's pregnancy, however, and of her desire for an abortion, he began to suffer from nervous diarrhoea. As he contemplated what might be possible with regard to this desperate, vulnerable young woman, he was in a state of heightened tension. His body was reacting to the turmoil in his mind.

After the trial, emotional tension of another kind seized him. In the summer of 1950, the house was put on the market. As Kitchener had now moved out, the Christies had the run of the place, and a new landlord was a threat. He might discover skeletal remains in the garden. It was not only Muriel Eady's femur that had worked its way to the surface; when her skull also appeared, Christie dropped it into a bombed house nearby.

One prospective buyer, Ernest McNeil, recalled how Christie had tried to deter him by telling him the house had a sinister past. McNeil was not in the least worried: he had once worked as an undertaker. Christie was visibly shaken to hear this. McNeil then asked a question that the police should have put: if two decomposing bodies had been in the wash-house for a length of time, why had Christie's dog not smelled them?

A surveyor's report concluding that the house was filthy, decaying and infested with bedbugs decided McNeil against buying 10 Rillington Place. It was bought instead by Charles Brown, a Jamaican, who moved black tenants into the empty flats. The Christies were horrified. They looked upon West Indian immigrants as inferior in every way and hated sharing the lavatory with them. Terrified that one of them might stumble on human remains, Christie went to the Poor Man's Law Centre in North Kensington, demanding protection from intrusion and clinging to exclusive use of the garden.

There were some positive developments. That summer Christie found a new job as a clerk for British Road Services. He settled in with his colleagues and even refereed some of their football matches. Medical records show that his health improved. After complaining of loss of memory in June 1950 he did not return to Dr Odess for almost a year, which was highly unusual.

MARRIAGE DISSOLVED

Life at home, however, continued to be fraught with problems. Christie and his wife were trapped in a house in which they were the senior tenants yet lacking any of the respect they felt due to them. Friction with the other inhabitants increased and, as she was at home all the time, Ethel bore the brunt of it. Christie wanted her to visit relatives in Sheffield more often so that he could enjoy her absence, but she declined to do so: they were under each other's feet more than ever in their small flat.

This raises the question of the dynamic between husband and wife. How much did Ethel Christie know? When she agreed to live with him after a gap of almost a decade, she was aware that he was a common criminal with aggressive tendencies. Yet he apparently mended his ways and she was proud of his wartime work as a reserve policeman. She did not realize that during that time he had an affair with a female colleague, visited prostitutes and strangled two women in the flat. Ethel knew about Beryl Evans's pregnancy and about Christie's plan to assist her, but she never connected an attempted abortion with murder. Her lies on her husband's behalf were not told to save him from the gallows; it never occurred to her that Christie was a killer. She believed—with good reason—that Timothy Evans had murdered his wife and baby. The only thing Christie had done, in her view, was to offer help to a young woman in distress out of kindness. He might rule the roost at home but Ethel still considered him 'a good man'. It was not simply blind loyalty that made her defend him against Mrs Probert's accusations: she was describing honestly the husband with whom she had lived for many years in comparative harmony.

Having grown accustomed to his regular bouts of illness, Ethel was pleased when Christie no longer felt the need to visit a doctor. In fact, it was Ethel herself who called on Dr Odess to ask for sleeping tablets. Disputes with the other tenants over their respective rights had made her nervous and depressed. At one point, she had had to take a fellow tenant to court for assault.

Tensions within 10 Rillington Place eventually told on Christie as well. In the spring of 1952, his anxiety attacks returned. A number of factors were at work. First, he was no longer the master of the house. Even though he was only a tenant, Christie had always acted as the gatekeeper and substitute landlord. He and Ethel were now hostages in what they saw as a black ghetto, too poor to leave premises in which their quality of life had markedly deteriorated. Also, there was no longer any sexual pleasure in the marriage. Since the execution of Timothy Evans, the Christies had not had intercourse. Though it had only been sporadic at best, Ethel missed it and teased her husband about his impotence, which rankled deeply.

But underpinning Christie's other anxieties was the fear of being found out: of being revealed as a vicious serial killer who had murdered a man's wife and child then framed him for the crimes. And if the skeletons of his two earlier victims were ever unearthed, he would be the obvious murder suspect because he was the only person to have worked in the garden.

Growing stress sent Christie back to Dr Odess. Although there were physical symptoms — diarrhoea, fibrositis and catarrh — he was diagnosed as having an anxiety state and referred to a specialist at St Charles' Hospital. During the three weeks that Christie was under observation as an in-patient, he was described as being highly neurotic. In July, he was sent to Springfield Mental Hospital, where he made the startling and ridiculous claim that his ailments had started when he was accused by Evans of committing two murders. Dr Dinshaw Petit thought him so unstable that he recommended a stay at the hospital as an in-patient. Christie refused, arguing that his wife would be alarmed to be left alone in the house with so many black people. When he visited Petit again in August, Christie insisted that he was much better, even though he was clearly disturbed. Regular visits to Dr Odess continued, but treatment for physical symptoms could not cure Christie's serious psychological problems.

Cumulative pressures built throughout the autumn and reached a point where they demanded release. Early in December, Christie gave in his notice, claiming that he had been offered a better job in Sheffield. Eight days later, he strangled his wife in bed with one of her stockings. He would later insist that it was a mercy killing, but he had obeyed other promptings: Christie was an unstable man, living in two dingy rooms with a depressed woman whose presence curbed his licence to roam for

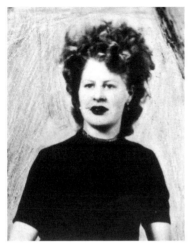

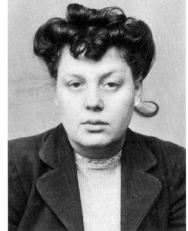

13 *Above*: Christie's sixth victim, Rita Nelson. (HO 291/228)

14 *Above right*: Kathleen Maloney, the seventh victim. (HO 291/228)

15 *Right*: The eighth and last victim Hectorina Maclennan, whose corpse was the first to be found in the kitchen at Rillington Place. (HO 291/228)

METROPOLITAN POLICE

Reference { C.O. 201/53/62
to papers { Divl.　　　　　　　Notting Hill STATION. 'F' DIVN.

Registry Folio No. 21/24/63C　　　　26th March　　195 3

To: Chief Superintendent

At 5 p.m., on the 24th March, 1953, Police were
called to 10, Rillington Place, Notting Hill, W.11, and
discovered the bodies of four adult females. The
bodies were later removed to Kensington Mortuary where
Post Mortem examinations were carried out by Doctor
F.E. Camps. In each case the cause of death was
apparently due to strangulation.

Briefly, the facts are that the ground floor flat
at this address was occupied by John Reginald Halliday
CHRISTIE, C.R.O. No.7720/21, who left the address on
Thursday, 19th March, 1953, having disposed of his
furniture about a month earlier.

The premises are owned by Mr. Charles BROWN, a man
of colour, of 26, Silchester Terrace, London, W.11, who
arranged for a Mr. Beresford BROWN, who lived on the
top floor of this three storied house, to take over the
ground floor flat. During the afternoon of Tuesday,
24th March, the latter, whilst doing some repairs in the
kitchen, pulled some wall-paper away in the corner of
the room and discovered a wood partition. He tore part
of the wall-paper away and found a small hole in the

17 *Left*: Christie's kitchen, showing the papered-over alcove where the women's bodies were uncovered. (MEPO 2/9535)

18 *Below*: The front room with the floorboards removed: Ethel Christie's body was found beneath them. (MEPO 2/9535)

16 *Left*: Metropolitan Police memo reporting the discovery of the four Rillington Place bodies on 24 March 1953. (MEPO 3/3147)

19 *Above*: John Christie arriving for his second appearance at West London's magistrates' court under police custody.

20 *Right*: Christie's statement on 5 June 1953 confessing to the murders of Ruth Fuerst and Muriel Eady; he did not volunteer this information until he learnt that bodies had been found in his garden. (MEPO 2/9535)

3

Continuation of Statement of John Regnald, Halliday Christie

her, I strangled her with a piece of
rope. I remember urine and excretta
coming away from her. She was
completely naked. I tried to put
some of her clothes back on her.
She had a leopard skin coat and
I wrapped this round her. I took her
from the bedroom into the front
room and put her under the
floor boards. I had to do that
because of my wife coming back. I
put the remainder of her clothing
under the floor boards too. My
wife came home in the evening
My brother-in-law, Mr. Waddington
came with her. Mr. Waddington
went back home the next day and
during the afternoon my wife went
out. I think she was working at
Osrams. While she was out I
pulled the ~~board~~ body up from
under the floor boards and took
it into the outhouse (The washhouse)
Late in the day I dug a hole in
the garden and in the evening
when it was dark, about 10 o'clock
I should say, I put the body down
in the hole and covered it up quickly

Signature ..... JR Christie

Signature
witnessed by .....

Use both sides if necessary. (If this is done, *both* sides of the form must be signed and witnessed).
M.P. 46235/60,000 Jan./1952 w126 (4)

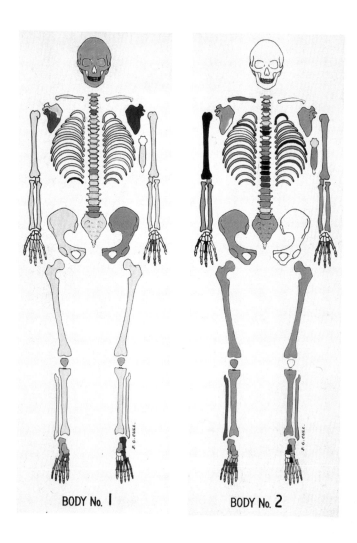

BODY No. 1

BODY No. 2

21 *Left*: The skeletons from the garden of 10 Rillington Place: colour coding was used to show where different bones had been recovered. (DPP 2/2246)

22 *Right*: The reconstituted skulls of Ruth Fuerst and Muriel Eady. (DPP 2/2246)

23 *Below*: Press article appealing for information on missing women Fuerst and Eady after the discovery of bodies in Christie's garden. (MEPO 2/9535)

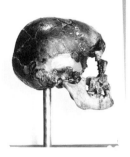

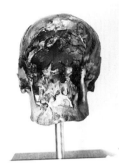

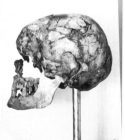

24/64. CHRISTIE, John Reginald Halliday, aged 55 years
Central Criminal Court
Murder
No. 1 in the Calendar

I attended the trial of the above-named prisoner at the Central Criminal Court on the 22nd, 23rd, 24th and 25th June, 1953.

Dr. Jack A Hobson gave evidence for the defence on the lines of his report, a copy of which is attached.

I was called in rebuttal and gave evidence on the lines of my report to the Court, a copy of which is attached.

Dr. Desmond Curran was also called in rebuttal and gave evidence on the lines of his report, the original of which was sent to the Prison Commissioners.

Throughout the trial no new aspect of the prisoner's mental condition emerged except that on Wednesday, 24th June, 1953, at the luncheon adjournment, when Christie was being escorted out of the dock to the cells below, The Hospital Officer in charge of prisoner, Mr. Heaney, quite properly guided him down to the cells by touching Christie's arm; when Mr. Heaney did this, Christie immediately turned round and in a vicious state said: "Take your bloody hands off me." It was some minutes before Christie settled but after he did he apologised for his conduct.

Each day when I saw him at the Court before trial commenced and after the trial had been adjourned, and at the luncheon adjournment, Christie appeared always alert and appeared to be well in touch with his position.

When I saw him after he had been condemned I saw no marked change in him. He was affable and polite and showed no anxiety nor distress of mind.

As a possible explanation of this prisoner's abnormal conduct I offer the following speculation based on the following points:

    1. As a boy he had a strict and somewhat domineering father.
    2. As a youth he found himself sexually very immature as compared with his adolescent companions.
    3. The reported incident when he was impotent with a girl of about his own age and the resulting teasing which he received from his male friends and female friends gave him a feeling of inferiority and helped to decrease his sexual potency.
    4. His alleged impotency with his wife for the first 2½-3 years of marriage.
    5. His conduct with prostitutes when he was acting as a War Reserve Police Officer.

24 *Left*: Report from Dr J.C. Matheson, principal medical officer at Brixton prison, describing Christie's behaviour during his trial. He goes on to say that 'a Statutory Enquiry should be held in view of the marked abnormalities which this prisoner displays'. (PCOM 9/1668)

25 *Right*: Timothy Evans's official pardon on 18 October 1966. (CRIM 1/2116) new victims. Tensions between them were high, and in taunting him about his impotence, Ethel had rubbed salt in his wounds.

What exactly triggered the moment of violence we shall never know, but Christie must have used great strength. Ethel was not subdued by drink or rendered defenceless by coal gas. She was an able woman of 54 who would have resisted the attack. Unlike his other adult victims, Ethel was not killed in a sexual frenzy; no intercourse took place afterwards.

Unsure what to do with her, Christie left her in bed for a couple of days. He then put the corpse in a flannel blanket, covered the head with a pillow case, and wrapped a silk night-gown and flowered dress around it. He hid his wife's body under the floorboards in the front room. 'I thought that was the best way to lay her to rest,' he said (MEPO 2/9535). He now had to explain her disappearance. Conflicting excuses were given to various neighbours, but Ethel's relatives in Sheffield posed the real problem. They would expect Christmas cards written by her.

A card was sent to the Bartles (his sister-in-law and her husband) signed 'From Ethel and Reg', and a letter enclosed by Christie claiming that his wife had been unable to write because of rheumatism in her fingers (see plate 12). He had earlier forwarded a letter to Lily Bartle, written by Ethel shortly before her death. Christie changed the date to the day after the murder and sent it in an envelope that he addressed himself, explaining that he had sent it from work. The Bartles did not know he was unemployed.

To get money, Christie sold his wife's watch and wedding ring to a jewellery shop. Early in the New Year, he sold his furniture to Robert Hookway for £12. All that remained was an old mattress, two chairs, a kitchen table and the deckchair used in the murder of Muriel Eady. The chair would soon host other victims.

THREE MORE VICTIMS

Christie was by now a pathetic figure, shivering in his barely furnished flat with only his mongrel bitch, Judy, and his cat for company. To control the stink of Ethel's decomposing body, he regularly disinfected the place with Jeyes' fluid. His weekly income from the employment exchange was £2 14s. Needing more money, he plundered his wife's savings account by forging her signature to gain £10 15s 2d. It was a miserable existence, but it left him free to search for other victims.

Christie was later confused about names and dates, but it seems that the first woman he lured back to Rillington Place was Rita Nelson (see plate 13), a blonde prostitute in her twenties from Belfast with convictions for larceny, soliciting and drunkenness. Nelson was working at Lyons' tea shop when it was discovered she was 24 weeks pregnant. Not wishing to return to Northern Ireland in that condition, she was referred by the firm's medical officer to the Samaritan Hospital for Women, but never turned up for her appointment.

Christie would later claim that Nelson abused him in

the street, followed him home and started a fight. It is more likely that he convinced her that he could give her an abortion because he put her in his deckchair, used his inhalation device to subdue her with gas, then strangled her with a piece of rope deliberately left within reach. The post-mortem vaginal swab revealed the presence of sperm. After trussing the corpse up as he had those of Beryl Evans and his wife, he pulled away a small cupboard in the kitchen and stuffed Nelson into the alcove.

On 19 January 1953, Nelson's landlady reported her missing to the police — so the murder must have occurred shortly before then. At that time Christie was already acquainted with his next victim, Kathleen Maloney (see plate 14), a brown haired woman in her mid-twenties. Maloney was an orphan who had absconded from the convent in which she was bought up. A heavy drinker, she was well known to the police as a prostitute and had a number of illegitimate children. Three weeks before Christmas, she and another prostitute accompanied Christie to a room where he had taken nude pictures of the second woman while Maloney watched. Christie met Maloney again in a pub and later took her to his flat, where she sat down in his deckchair.

As his victim was fairly drunk, it would not have been difficult for Christie to overpower her. He made her inhale the gas, strangled her with his rope and had intercourse, then put a diaper between her legs — the first cloth to hand — to catch the discharge. He then went to bed. When he awoke next morning, he found her still lying in the deckchair. Wrapping her body in a blanket and putting a pillowcase over her head, he shoved her into the alcove with her legs vertical against the wall.

It is probable that Christie saw Margaret Forrest as his next victim. He met her in the Panda Café in Westbourne Park Road; trawling through the squalid cafés in the area was his way of finding prostitutes and/or victims. Forrest suffered from migraines and might well have ended up in the deckchair inhaling Christie's gas. Impressed by his putative medical expertise, she made an appointment to visit him for treatment for her catarrh. As in the case of Muriel Eady, this would have involved the inhalation device. When Forrest failed to turn up for the appointment, Christie went in search of her and complained; she agreed to come to the house later but lost the address. For once, the killer was thwarted.

He had more success with Hectorina Maclennan (see plate 15), a brunette of 26 who had come to London in 1948 with her parents. The Maclennans returned to Scotland four years later and took their daughter's two illegitimate children with them, leaving her free to continue her precarious life as a prostitute in the capital. When Christie met her in a café in March, she was depressed because she could not find a flat. Christie told her that he might help and agreed to meet her later outside Ladbroke Grove station. He was dismayed when she turned up with her boyfriend, Alex Baker, an unemployed lorry driver estranged from his wife.

Reluctantly, Christie showed them his flat. He explained

that he was expecting a transfer from work soon; his furniture had been sent on to his new address. When they left, Baker and Maclennan firmly believed they had been offered the flat. Arriving back at their lodgings, they found they had been locked out, and returned to Rillington Place. Though Christie could hardly have wanted guests in a flat that contained three murder victims, he agreed to put them up. Refusing to let them sleep together, he sat up all night in the kitchen with Maclennan while Baker had use of the mattress. For three nights, he watched the young woman doze off in the deckchair, feasting his eyes on her and making his murderous plans.

Glad to get rid of the couple at last, he was keen to entice Maclennan back to Rillington Place alone. He turned up at the labour exchange where Baker went in search of a job and spoke to Maclennan alone, inviting her to return to the flat. His pretext for making the offer is not known, but she agreed. There was no secrecy about it: she told Baker where she was going.

When Maclennan arrived, Christie waved her to the deckchair and made her a drink. As he took the clip off the gas pipe, however, she saw him and became alarmed. But Christie's killing routine was by now well practised: he held her down, applied the gas, strangled her with a rope and had intercourse. Afraid that Baker would call at any moment, he did not bother to use a diaper or put her in a blanket; instead he bundled her unceremoniously into the alcove and hooked her brassiere to Maloney's legs which were still vertical against the wall. The cupboard door was slammed on its gruesome jumble of bodies.

Baker called late that afternoon. His girlfriend had not turned up at the café where they had agreed to meet. All he knew was that she was visiting Rillington Place. Christie said that she had never arrived, and invited Baker to search the flat, making him a cup of tea to calm him down. Baker noticed an unpleasant smell, but could not identify it. Expressing concern about Maclennan's disappearance, Christie actually joined Baker in a pointless search of the streets, and for the next few days met him at the labour exchange to ask for any news of the missing woman.

Events now speeded up. Short of money, Christie was eager to sub-let the flat, even though he had no right to do so. A Mr and Mrs Reilly agreed to take it, and he persuaded them to pay £7 13s rent in advance. Borrowing a suitcase from Reilly, he then left with his meagre possessions. When Charles Brown, the landlord, called that evening he was astonished to find new tenants in the flat. Not only had Christie taken money from them fraudulently, he was several weeks behind with his rent. Brown let the Reillys stay the night, but they left next day.

Beresford Brown, a tenant occupying one of the rooms in Evans's old flat, was given permission to use the kitchen on the ground floor, and on 24 March went in to put up brackets to hold a wireless set. When he tapped on one wall, he heard a hollow sound and realized there must be a concealed alcove. Ripping off the wallpaper, he peered inside with the aid of a torch, and saw the naked body of Hectorina Maclennan. Brown quickly called another tenant, Ivan Williams, who looked into the alcove and confirmed the presence of a dead body.

Brown raced off to the police station. A police search was made of Rillington Place: the bodies of Maclennan, Maloney and Nelson were taken from the alcove, and Ethel Christie's body was discovered beneath the floorboards (see plates 16, 17 and 18). When the garden was later searched, the skeletal remains of Fuerst and Eady were unearthed (see plates 21 and 22).

Christie was now the target of a nationwide manhunt. Displaying his photograph, newspapers warned that a serial killer was on the loose, and asked the question that was soon on everyone's minds: when would the monster strike again?

In fact, all that Christie did was to wander aimlessly around London. On 31 March, he was seen on the embankment near Putney Bridge by Police Constable Thomas Ledger. Christie claimed that he was John Waddington (Ethel's brother-in-law's name), but had no means of proving his identity. Ledger asked him to remove his hat and the distinctive bald head of John Reginald Halliday Christie came into view.

It was all over, but the intense public relief was tinged with disappointment. Having been built up in the press as an uncontrollable serial killer, Christie had surrendered meekly to a policeman, and some people felt cheated: there was no violence, no blood, no dramatic climax to his horrendous criminal career. The ravening beast had transformed himself back into a mild, harmless, respectable clerk.

CHAPTER FOUR

The Trial of John Christie

Christie's first statement was taken by Detective Inspector Kelly in the presence of Chief Inspector Griffin at Putney police station on 31 March 1953 (MEPO 2/9535; see plate 10). It began, characteristically, with a mention of his ill health. 'I have not been well for a long while, about eighteen months I have been suffering from fibrositis and enteritis. I had a breakdown in hospital.' His wife, he claimed, had been suffering from persecution by the black tenants at the house. On the morning of 14 December, he had awoken to find Ethel having convulsions. She began to choke. 'I did what I could to try to restore breathing but it was hopeless. It appeared too late to call for assistance. That's when I couldn't bear to see her, so I got a stocking and tied it round her neck to put her to sleep.' A brutal murder was made to sound like a marital favour.

Christie said that he noticed his bottle of pheno-barbitone tablets had only two out of twenty-five left. 'I knew then she must have taken the remainder.' This claim of a suicide attempt was disproved by the post-mortem on Ethel Christie, which found no trace of the drug.

Unable to accept the horror of what he had done to his wife, Christie had tried to portray it as an act of mercy by a caring husband, and there was similar distortion with regard to the murders of Rita Nelson, Kathleen Maloney and Hectorina Maclennan. The first was described as a case of self-defence against a prostitute who demanded money from him in the street or she would 'scream and say I had interfered with her'. Christie said that when he opened the door to the house:

> she forced her way in. I went to the kitchen and she was still on about this thirty shillings. I tried to get her out and she picked up a frying pan to hit me. I closed with her and there was a struggle and she fell back on the chair. It was a deck chair. There was a piece of rope hanging from the chair. I don't remember what happened but I must have gone haywire. The next thing I remember she was lying still in the chair with the rope around her neck.

He omitted to mention that he had deliberately placed the rope on the chair beforehand.

Kathleen Maloney, he claimed, had come to look at his flat with a view to taking it over:

> She said it would be suitable subject to the landlord's permission. It was then she made suggestions that she would visit me for a few days. She said this so that I would use my influence with the landlord. I was rather annoyed and told her it didn't interest me. I think she started saying I was making

accusations against her when she saw there was nothing doing. She said she would bring someone down to me.

Christie did his best to portray himself as a victim, offered sexual favours in return for helping the woman to secure the flat and then, when he refused on moral grounds, threatened with violence. 'I remember she started fighting. I am very quiet and avoid fighting. I know there was something, it's in the back of my mind. She was on the floor. I must have put her in the alcove straight away.'

The two women are not named in the statement, but Christie seems to have thought that Kathleen Maloney was the first victim. Yet it was Rita Nelson who was last discovered in the alcove and therefore first to be put there. Christie's confusion is understandable: in the week before his arrest he was in a daze, hungry, almost penniless and — after a short stay in Rowton House, a hostel for down-and-outs — living rough while the police hunted him. What he could not admit was that Maloney was a prostitute invited back to his flat for sex and that Nelson had been tricked into believing he would perform an illegal abortion on her.

Hectorina Maclennan's murder was described as an accident. Christie explained that she and her boyfriend had stayed with him. 'I told them they would have to go as he [Baker] was being very unpleasant. He told me the police were looking for her for some offence.' According to Christie, Maclennan returned alone that night and insisted on staying in case Baker came — but Christie told her to go. 'She was very funny about it. I got hold of her arm to try to lead her out. I pushed her out of the kitchen. She started struggling like anything and some of her clothing got torn. She then sort of fell limp.' Falling limp was his euphemism for being violently strangled to death.

> She sank to the ground and I think some of her clothing must have caught around her neck in the struggle. She was just out of the kitchen in the passage way. I tried to lift her up but couldn't. I then pulled her into the kitchen on to a chair. I felt her pulse, but it wasn't beating. I pulled the cupboard away and must have put her in there.

The statement does not mention that gas and a rope were used in all three cases, nor that intercourse took place during or immediately after the murders. It was left to the post-mortems to provide these salient details.

A further statement was appended. 'I wish to state that I am grateful to the police in charge for the kindly way in which I have been treated at Putney Station. There has been no act of any kind to force me to say and do anything.' The note of ingratiation is characteristic. As Christie had not been challenged about the human remains found in the garden at Rillington Place, he volunteered no information about his first two victims. It was not until 5 June that he gave a second statement to Kelly and Griffin from Brixton prison, formally responding to the news that human bones had been dug up in his garden by confessing to the murders of Ruth Fuerst and Muriel Eady (see plate 23).

Prison revived Christie. He had food, shelter and freedom from the ordeal of fending for himself with no resources. He also had the status of a serial killer, and enjoyed the perverted respect of other inmates as a result. Christie compared himself to the notorious John George Haigh, the acid bath murderer, who had been hanged in August 1949. Feeling more confident, he was more precise and detailed in his second statement (MEPO 2/9535; see plate 20). With regard to Ruth Fuerst, he presented himself once more as having been the victim of a headstrong prostitute:

> One day when this Austrian girl was with me in the flat at No. 10 Rillington Place, she undressed and wanted me to have sex with her. I got a telegram while she was there saying that my wife was on her way home. The girl wanted us to team up together and go right away somewhere together. I could not do that.

He confessed to having intercourse and strangling her, yet still believed there were extenuating circumstances. It was Fuerst who wanted to have sex with him, making her the initiator. Christie's claim that she urged him to run away with her was ludicrous.

Muriel Eady was at least spared gross misrepresentation. Christie admitted that she came 'by appointment when my wife was out'. He explained how his inhalation device worked:

> She inhaled the stuff from the tube. I did it to make her dopey. She became sort of unconscious and I have a vague recollection

of getting a stocking and tying it round her neck, I am not too clear about this. It may have been the Austrian girl [Fuerst] that I used gas on. I don't think it was both. I believe I had intercourse with her at the time I strangled her.

The first person to whom Christie confessed that he had killed Beryl Evans was a psychiatrist. On 27 April, Dr J.A. Hobson of the Middlesex Hospital interviewed him in prison. 'I felt really bad about that, sir,' said Christie sadly. 'I must have been intimate with her then strangled her' (CAB 143/13). There was no mention of his being incapacitated by fibrositis and enteritis at the time.

It was in his third statement, made in prison in the presence of Kelly and Griffin on 8 June, that Christie made a formal confession to Beryl's murder (MEPO 2/9535; see plate 6). As in the case of his wife, he disguised a gruesome murder as a mercy killing, claiming in his statement that Beryl Evans had told him that her husband was 'knocking her about and that she was going to make an end of it, meaning that she was going to commit suicide'. Christie claimed that he saved her from gassing herself but said nothing about it to his wife as Beryl had asked him to be discreet. 'When I went up to Mrs. Evans the next day at lunch time, she begged me to help her go through with it, meaning to help her commit suicide. She said she would do anything if I would help her. I think she was referring to letting me be intimate with her.'

This is a grotesque claim about a frightened young woman who was desperate to have an abortion and who made the mistake of trusting Christie to perform it. Why else had he gone upstairs that day? Admitting that he tried to have intercourse after strangling Beryl, he fell back on his old excuse of suffering from fibrositis and enteritis: 'I was not physically capable.' Christie would later confess that he did have intercourse with her. On Evans's return that day, Christie went on, he told him that his wife had committed suicide. 'When I left Evans in the bedroom that Tuesday, he did not know that his wife had been strangled. He thought she had gassed herself.'

Even when faced with damning evidence against him, Christie could not tell the truth. There was no reference to abortion and he said that Evans, knowing he might be suspected of murder, had decided to put his wife's body in his van and drive somewhere to dispose of it. Christie never confessed to the murder of Geraldine. Indeed, in this third statement, he tried to pass himself off as a potential adoptive parent: 'My wife and I had a chat and we agreed between us that if they [the Evanses] did separate we would adopt the baby.' Yet whoever killed the mother killed the child as well. Why else were they found in exactly the same place, and murdered in the same way?

In all, Christie made at least four confessions to the murder of Beryl Evans, changing the details each time. But he would say nothing about Geraldine. To have killed seven women and to have had sexual relations with six of them at the time gave him a freakish glamour in prison. Had other inmates known that he had also strangled a child in cold blood, Christie would have been despised rather than admired, and his personal safety would have been at risk.

Christie saw himself as an essentially decent man led astray by women. He could not destroy that image in his mind by admitting to the murder of a child. While he was awaiting execution, Mrs Probert sent him a heartfelt letter, begging him to clear his conscience by confessing to the murder of Geraldine, thereby freeing her son from any taint:

> You are where my boy was three years ago. He knew what was waiting for him and there was no turning back so only the truth would do. He told the priest the truth of his innocence and I will tell you what he said to me the last time I saw him. Mum I loved them I swear before God I never touched them. You did say half the truth last week when you told the Judge you killed poor Beryl but only the whole truth will save you from the wrath of God. (CAB 143/20)

Christie ignored her plea.

During their search at Rillington Place, the police had found a tobacco tin containing four sets of pubic hair. After he had signed his third statement, Christie added that 'it came from the three women in the alcove and my wife. I feel certain of this but I can't remember when or how I took it.' In fact, none of the pubic hair matched that of the three prostitutes or Ethel Christie. When Beryl Evans was exhumed, her pubic hair was also ruled out. The hair must have been gathered elsewhere. Christie often boasted in prison about other victims, although this may have been simply an attempt to impress. We will never learn if these trophies were collected while the women in question were alive or dead.

PUBLIC NOTORIETY

In view of the position it came to hold in British legal history, the trial of Timothy Evans in 1950 had little impact at the time. The opposite was the case with John Christie: his crimes became public sensations. The whole of the front page of the *Sunday Pictorial* on 26 April 1953 was given over to a banner headline, a 'confession' by Christie ghostwritten by the journalist who interviewed him, and a photograph of Christie and his dog in the garden at Rillington Place. The prisoner went out of his way to say how considerate prison staff had been. Sweets, apples and cigarettes were his favourite treats. 'At present I occupy a small room and am glad to be alone to settle a bit as I am still somewhat "fuddled" and dazed.'

After talking about his life in prison and asking to be remembered to any old acquaintances, Christie signed off with another reference to his health. 'I would like to keep on writing but it is at the moment difficult to put one's thoughts into words and my head is aching rather badly.' But his headache was not caused by remorse. Using selective memory, he managed to forget unsavoury details such as the sexual fury with which he had strangled and ravished six different women, and the clinical efficiency used in killing his wife and snuffing out the life of a small child.

While in Brixton, Christie was examined by psychiatrists. They all disliked him, finding him a creepy, unpleasant, snivelling creature. When Christie was later moved to Pentonville, clinical psychologist Stephen H. Coates summed him up: 'A sad, unhappy, rather anxiety-ridden little man, with a sufficiently well-structured personality to have survived life on a circumscribed narrow level. Probably with many slight psychosomatic or hysterical complaints. A good deal of repression, especially of aggression. Probably he's happier in male society.' (PCOM 9/1668)

The trial of John Christie for the murder of his wife opened in No. 1 Court at the Old Bailey on 22 June 1954 (the transcript can be read in DPP 2/2246). Mr Justice Finnemore was the judge. The Crown was represented by the Attorney-General, Sir Lionel Heald, and his team. Leading the defence was Derek Curtis-Bennett. The list of prosecution witnesses included various people to whom Christie had lied about his wife's whereabouts, furniture dealer Robert Hookway, the jeweller who had bought Ethel's watch and ring, Dr Odess, Chief Inspector Griffin and Alex Baker, the friend of Hectorina Maclennan. A key witness was Dr Francis Camps, who performed the post-mortems on the four bodies. There was a lot of evidence against Christie, as we have already seen, but securing a guilty verdict was not as simple as anticipated.

On the second day, it was the turn of the defence. Curtis-

Bennett argued that Christie was insane and that he did not know that he was doing wrong when he committed the crimes. There was a surge of interest as the prisoner was called to the witness box. The court was packed and many applications to attend had been turned down, although among those present were Terence Rattigan and the American playwright Robert Sherwood.

One of the most perceptive observers was Ronald Maxwell, a young journalist who would later write a full account in *The Christie Case*. Maxwell recalled how Christie walked jerkily from the dock to the witness box and stood there for a full 30 seconds, looking at the wording of the oath: 'He appeared to be crying... The room was completely silent, as Christie fidgeted, and then mumbled the oath.' His voice was so quiet that he was advised to move to the corner of the box so that his words might carry better. Curtis-Bennett drew the story of his life out of him. 'Christie looked and sounded like a rather meek, henpecked husband when he said he had been very happy with his wife,' noted Maxwell.

Asked about his relationship with Ruth Fuerst, the prisoner replied, 'She just said that she was rather inclined to be affectionate towards me.' Christie said that he could not remember if the Austrian woman had been his first victim. 'May you have done more killings than you are going to tell us?' asked Curtis-Bennett. 'I can't say exactly,' replied Christie. 'I might have done.' When he talked about his victims, his account of each roughly matched that given in his statements. Showing little emotion over the deaths of the others, he wept freely when he gave evidence about his wife.

When the trial resumed next morning, a microphone had been fitted in the witness box and Christie's voice was much clearer. What he could not provide were motives for the killings. Curtis-Bennett pressed him about the murder of Beryl Evans, but Christie seemed to think it no different to any of the other murders. The judge asked him why, in his first statement to the police on 31 March, he had not mentioned Fuerst, Eady and Beryl Evans. Christie claimed he had dismissed them from his mind, and of Beryl's death he said, 'I never gave it another thought.'

> 'You say that you killed Mrs Evans,' said the judge, 'you had discussed with her husband about disposing of her body and the danger he stood in. He was charged with her murder and the murder of the little child. You gave evidence in a murder trial in this court. Do you mean that you had forgotten all that?'
> 'Yes, sir,' replied Christie, 'it had gone clean out of my mind.'

This was a lie: among the items found in his wallet at the time of his arrest was a newspaper cutting about the evidence he had given at Evans's trial.

Cross-examined by the Attorney-General, Christie was asked why he had put his wife under the floorboards. 'I did not want to be separated from her or lose her,' said Christie, 'and that is why I still had her in the house.' According to Maxwell, he seemed a little pleased with himself when he said this. 'If there had been a policeman present when you killed your wife,'

Sir Lionel asked, 'would you have done it?' Christie's reply was significant: 'I do not suppose so.' In other words, he did know the difference between right and wrong, the very issue at stake. Sir Lionel reinforced the point by getting Christie to admit that he had deceived several people about the disappearance of his wife, showing that he knew what he had done was wrong and was trying to cover his tracks.

After three hours in the witness box, Christie was replaced by Dr J.A. Hobson, the psychiatrist called by the defence. Having seen Christie ten or twelve times, Hobson believed that he was suffering from a disease of the mind within the terms of the McNaughten Rules (which set the precedent for a verdict of guilty but insane) and was unaware that what he did was wrong: 'I felt throughout that he has been unable to remember things, he has falsely remembered things. I believe that most of the time this falsification of memory or his forgetting resulted from hysteria…' Hobson added that Christie had tried his best to be co-operative but that 'these tricks of memory, or avoidance of getting down to disturbing topics, is to preserve his own self-respect … rather than to avoid incriminating himself'.

By way of rebuttal, the prosecution called Dr J.C. Matheson, principal medical officer at Brixton prison (see plate 24), who said:

> He is, in my opinion, a man of weak character. He is immature, certainly, in his sexual life. He is a man who, in difficult times and in the face of problems, tends to exaggerate and act in an

hysterical fashion. He is not suffering from hysteria, but is a man with an hysterical personality who, in certain circumstances, behaves as a man suffering from hysteria would behave.

Dr D. Curran, psychiatrist at St George's Hospital, offered further comments:

> Christie was somewhat emotional, tremulous and fearful on admission but soon settled down. He has been meticulously clean and tidy in his person and habits; he has always kept himself well occupied; he has mixed freely with the other patients. He has been noticeably egocentric and conceited. He keeps a photograph of himself in his cell. He has been a great talker and seems to enjoy discussing his case, bringing the conversation round to it.

Curran added that he did not believe Christie's alleged loss of memory was genuine. 'He has a remarkable capacity for dismissing the unpleasant from his mind.' (The full medical and scientific reports can be seen in CAB 143/18.)

Concluding the case for the defence, Curtis-Bennett urged the jury to bring in a verdict of guilty but insane, citing the murder of Ethel Christie as an example of a motiveless and purposeless crime:

> His wife was the person he loved best in the world. I suggest that this is maniacal behaviour, this sex indignity imposed by him on some of these women. You may think that a man who has intercourse with a dead or dying body is mad, and that I think has been proved here on one occasion at least.

Sir Lionel rose for the prosecution. 'We have to prove,' he told the jury, 'and have very clearly proved, that Christie did deliberately and intentionally kill his wife on 14 December. He killed her by strangling her with a stocking, and he knew perfectly well what he was doing.' He stressed the point made by Dr Curran that sex perversion was not necessarily proof of insanity, and argued that it was possible to give a motive for the murder of Ethel Christie. When he dealt with the Evans case, he made the strange remark that there was no reason to think that Christie had killed the baby as well. With enough already on his plate, he implied, there was no need to add that charge to his list of crimes.

Sifting the evidence with scrupulous care, Mr Justice Finnemore spoke for nearly two and a half hours. He said that because 'a man acted like a monster', it did not mean that he was insane, noting the question asked by Sir Lionel about whether Christie would have killed if there had been a policeman in the room. Christie's reply, observed the judge, had been that of a sane man. At the end of his summing-up, he directed the jury to retire to consider their verdict.

Christie did not agonize about their decision: while he waited in the cell below the dock, he asked for the score in the Test match. The jury returned after 85 minutes and found him guilty of the murder of his wife. Asked if he had anything to say about why the court should not give judgement of death according to the law, Christie remained silent. With the black cap in place, the judge, visibly moved, pronounced the death sentence. It was Thursday 25 June 1953: nearly ten years since Christie had murdered his first known victim.

There was no appeal against the sentence. Less than a month later, on 15 July, Christie was hanged in Pentonville Prison by Albert Pierrepoint, the same public executioner who had despatched Timothy Evans to his undeserved grave.

The two men differed so markedly in age, appearance and intelligence that it is easy to overlook the similarities between them. Both grew up in households where the female influence dominated, and were frail children, protected by their mothers. Both spent their childhoods in dismal surroundings: Christie's house looked out on a graveyard while Evans was born in the shadow of a colliery. Both had a Christian upbringing that they later renounced. Both were sensitive men with strong emotions. Both visited prostitutes. Christie was a serial adulterer and Evans was unfaithful to his wife. When roused, neither man had any concern for consequences. Both were seasoned liars. Both were dogged by ill health. Both had regional accents. Both had left their birthplaces for the uncertain promise of life in London. Each, in his own way, was a driven man.

Had their paths not crossed at 10 Rillington Place, it is certain that Evans's life would have taken a very different course. Christie, on the other hand, was always destined for the gallows. The shame of it was that he contrived to take an innocent man with him.

CHAPTER FIVE

Unsafe Conviction

In the wake of the trial, there was a predictable outcry. As Christie had confessed to the murder of Beryl Evans, the conviction of her husband was deemed to be unsafe: this raised the spectre that a man had been hanged in error. Under pressure from various sources, the Home Secretary, Sir David Maxwell Fyfe, announced in Parliament on 6 July 1953 that he had set up a special inquiry. John Scott Henderson QC was appointed to investigate doubts about Evans's guilt, while assisting the inquiry was George Blackburn, the Assistant Chief Constable of West Riding.

Both sides of the House welcomed the inquiry, but there was criticism of the fact that it would be held in private. It was also felt that in the short time allowed—barely a week—it would be impossible to conduct a thorough examination of all the relevant documents and all the material witnesses. The inquiry opened on Monday 6 July. On the following day, Bernard Gillis QC was instructed by solicitors acting on behalf of Mrs Probert to represent her interests. Gillis made immediate contact with Scott Henderson, but was not allowed to see him until Thursday 9 July.

Gillis asked to see evidence already taken from witnesses and requested an opportunity to cross-examine them. He also wanted to see a transcript of Evans's trial and to have the right to call witnesses whose names he presented. Scott Henderson refused the first two requests, and said of the third that the listed witnesses could be called but that Gillis would be unable to question them directly. Gillis was, however, permitted to submit questions in writing, although Scott Henderson reserved the right to decide if they should be asked. He was determined to exercise full control over the inquiry.

Evidence from over twenty witnesses was heard, but the most exasperating came from Christie himself. On 9 July, at Pentonville, he appeared before Scott Henderson, Blackburn, Gillis, Mr Peacock from the Treasury Solicitor's office, Christie's solicitor, Roy Arthur, Derek Curtis-Bennett, Evans's barrister Malcolm Morris and the governor and chief officer of the prison. Christie raised no objection to the presence of any of them. Blackburn warned him that he would be questioned about the death of Geraldine Evans but that there was no proof that Christie had killed her, thereby handing him an easy way to escape responsibility for the crime by denying it.

A week away from the date of his execution, Christie might have thought that he had nothing to lose by telling the truth. Instead, he took refuge in memory loss once more:

> You see [he said in answer to a question about the murders
> of Fuerst and Eady], it seems very funny; it may seem silly,

but it is not; the moment I get to myself, take for instance the
moment I get out of here, it does not matter if you question me.
If you question me for hours it will not matter. The moment I
get out of here by myself again it is completely gone. I do not
give it another thought, and that is how it has been right the
way through. (quotes from Scott Henderson Report,
HO 45/25652)

Loss of memory never seemed to trouble him in the presence
of other prisoners. He talked openly about his crimes to them.
Asked who first raised the question of the Evans case with
him, Christie agreed that his solicitor and a prison doctor had
mentioned it: 'First of all they put it point-blank to me, had I
any connection with it at all. Then when I said that I had not it
was suggested that there may be some similarity. They asked
me to think hard and see if I could recollect truly one way or
another.'

Scott Henderson pressed on. 'Did they point out that there
was a similarity: that the three women in the kitchen had been
strangled, and that the two Evanses had been strangled?'
Christie replied that they had. 'They explained that it was a
similarity. It meant that there were two stranglers in one house,
and that was something which was highly improbable. It could
happen, but it is very improbable.'

After denying that he killed the baby, he was asked if he
had anything to do with the death of Beryl Evans. Christie
responded,

Well, I am not sure. If somebody came up to me — this is what
I was going to mention previously — and told me that there is
definite proof that I had something to do with one or both of
them, I should accept it as being right, that I must have done it,
but I want to know the truth about it as much as you do.

For someone who wanted to know the truth, Christie was very
skilful at concealing it. His evidence was both evasive and
misleading, yet Scott Henderson seemed to take it at face value.
When his report was issued, he summarized his findings:

1. The case for the prosecution against Evans as presented to
   the jury was an overwhelming one.
2. Having considered the material now available relating to the
   deaths of Mrs. Evans and Geraldine Evans, I am satisfied
   that Evans was responsible for both.
3. Christie's statements that he was responsible for the death of
   Mrs. Evans were not only unreliable but untrue.

I have therefore to report that in my opinion there is no ground
for thinking that there may have been any miscarriage of
justice in the conviction of Evans for the murder of Geraldine
Evans.

This caused outrage. Roundly condemned as a whitewash, the
report was the subject of an impassioned debate in the House
of Commons on 29 July. Geoffrey Bing QC was scathing: 'It is
shot through with prejudices and evidence of irregularities…'
(*Hansard*, 29 July 1953). He complained that letters sent by Mrs

Probert and her daughter to Mrs Lynch had been published in full in an appendix, without their permission. Written in anger that had long subsided, they were highly damaging to Evans. Bing pointed out that Evans's guilt depended on two incredible coincidences. The first was that two murderers, living in the same house but acting independently, strangled women with a ligature, had intercourse with their victims, wrapped and trussed them up in identical ways, moved them around the house, then put the bodies in the wash-house. The second was as extraordinary as the first: that Evans had accused the one man in London who was strangling women in the identical way that he, Evans, had strangled his wife and child.

Stung by the volume and intensity of the criticism, Scott Henderson issued a supplementary report, which was presented to Parliament on 14 July. He defended his findings and tried to answer specific accusations made against them. For example, the police were exonerated from the charge of having retained the missing time sheet from the building firm that showed what Willis and Jones were doing at Rillington Place during the critical period.

At Evans's trial, Christie had claimed that he had been disabled by fibrositis on 8 November 1949 and was therefore unable to carry the dead body of a woman. Scott Henderson admitted that Dr Odess had deposed that the patient did not complain about fibrositis until days after the murder. He added that the doctor could not be certain if the pain could have resulted from abnormal strain a few days earlier. However, having raised the issue of the state of Christie's health at the time of the murder, Scott Henderson then dismissed it.

The supplementary report was as unconvincing as its predecessor, but it remained the official verdict on the matter. Both reports are as striking for their omissions as for their contents. Beginning with a presumption of guilt on Evans's behalf, Scott Henderson made little effort to prove his innocence in the light of new information. But he had been right about one thing: the case against Evans as presented to the jury at his trial was overwhelming. It would be wrong to blame them for a verdict made in good faith on the strength of limited facts. Had they known that the chief witness against Evans had already strangled at least two women to death, there would have been a different outcome; had Christie been exposed at the Welshman's trial as the liar, necrophile and killer that he was, four other victims would have escaped his clutches.

Scott Henderson claimed that Christie's confession to the murder of Beryl Evans was 'not only unreliable it was untrue'. He noted that Christie had talked of gassing his victim to subdue her, yet no trace of carbon monoxide was found during her postmortem. It never occurred to him that Christie had invented the story of the assisted suicide to make himself appear as a friend to whom she turned, and that he had, in fact, overpowered Beryl another way, that is by punching her in the face. Scott Henderson was adamant. 'Obviously a confession which is

obtained in the circumstances which I have outlined and which
is materially varied as Christie's was, cannot be accepted unless
it is corroborated from independent sources.'

If he attached no credibility to the confession relating to
Beryl Evans, why did Scott Henderson readily accept those
relating to the murders of Fuerst, Eady, Nelson, Maloney,
Maclennan and Ethel Christie? They were also materially varied
and without independent corroboration. 'I am satisfied,' said Scott
Henderson in his report, 'that Christie gradually came to the
conclusion that it would be helpful in his defence if he confessed
to the murder of Mrs Evans.' He quoted the phrase 'the more
the merrier', which had been used by Christie to the chaplain at
Pentonville, suggesting that the prisoner had 'gained the impression that it was necessary for him to confess to murders'.

Dr J.A. Hobson later contradicted this. In a letter to Michael
Eddowes, author of *The Man On Your Conscience*, he wrote
on 24 March 1955 that the phrase had come originally from
another prisoner. Discussing their respective cases, this prisoner had said enviously to Christie

> that he was very lucky in having killed so many, that if you kill
> enough, as in war, you were sure to get away with it, and that
> in a business like this it was a question of the more the merrier.
> I cannot remember when it was that Christie told me of this
> incident but I believe it was at a later interview than the one in
> which he described how he had killed Mrs Evans.

Hobson, called by the defence at Christie's trial, remembered him well:

> Christie was a pathological liar and had unparalleled facility for self-deception. It was always difficult to sort out fact from fantasy in the history he gave. I did feel, however, that in his account to me [of Beryl's murder] he was telling the truth to the best of his ability and the whole interview was one of the most reliable I had with him. He told me the story spontaneously, with very little prompting, factually, coolly and without histrionics.

At the trial of Timothy Evans, the prosecution had relied heavily on the testimony of Christie and his wife. The fact that Christie had been revealed as a serial killer invalidated almost all the evidence he gave in court in 1950. Yet the report retained a naïve faith in what Christie and Ethel had said under oath. No attempt was made to study Evans's behaviour after the death of his wife. If he had really been the killer, would he have remained in London for a few days and calmly carried on with his job? Would he have gone to Wales where he could easily have been traced? More to the point, would he have left Christie's name out of his first statement in Merthyr Tydfil police station if he meant to later accuse him of the murder?

It seems strange that Scott Henderson was prepared to accept Evans's confession, extracted from an exhausted man in the middle of the night, yet disregard Christie's confession to the same murder, made in more comfortable conditions to a psychiatrist in a face-to-face interview, and subsequently repeated to others. If Evans killed his wife in the heat of an argument about money, why did he keep the cuttings about the Setty murder, indicating premeditation? Evans had no possible motive for killing his daughter and, given his devotion to her, every reason not to. Christie, on the other hand, did: the second murder was a means of concealing the first.

CONTINUING CONTROVERSY

Arguments continued to rage over the case, countless articles appearing in newspapers, magazines and learned journals. As there was a general feeling that Evans had been hanged in error, the whole issue of capital punishment took on a new resonance. It was not long before books and pamphlets about the case began to appear. But further investigation was not encouraged by the Establishment: in *The Man On Your Conscience* by Michael Eddowes, the author complains that he was not allowed to see the full transcript of the trial of Timothy Evans, or some of the case documents, or any of the evidence taken by Scott Henderson at the inquiry.

Entertaining for the sake of argument the notion that Evans did kill his wife and child, Eddowes lists 21 amazing coincidences if this was so, beginning with the fact that in November 1949, 10 Rillington Place would have been occupied by two murderers, the only men in the house. Long before the end of the list, Eddowes has demonstrated that the coincidences were too powerful to lie within the realms of possibility. The book goes on to absolve Evans of guilt and to argue that Christie killed everyone whose body was found at the house.

Analysis of both cases appears in *The Trials of Timothy John Evans and John Reginald Halliday Christie* edited by F. Tennyson Jesse (1957) for the Notable British Trials series. This author also concludes that it was more likely that Christie killed Beryl and Geraldine Evans.

The most famous book on the subject is *10 Rillington Place* by Ludovic Kennedy (1961). It begins with an open letter to the then Home Secretary, outlining the reasons for an urgent review of the case and quoting people who believed that a miscarriage of justice had taken place. One of them was the Rt. Hon. James Chuter Ede, Home Secretary at the time of Evans's execution and the person who had written 'the law must take its course' on Evans's papers. In 1955, he said, 'I think the Evans case shows that, in spite of all that has been done since, a mistake was possible, and that, in the form in which the verdict was actually given on a particular case, a mistake was made.'

10 Rillington Place went on to become the standard version of events even though it was not recognized as such by the powers-that-be. In the winter of 1965, however, Sir Daniel Brabin, a High Court judge, reheard the case in public. The main hearings of the inquiry took over thirty days. When the Brabin Report was published by HMSO in 1966, its conclusion was that 'it was more probable than not that Evans killed his wife and that he did not kill his daughter'.

As Evans had been hanged for the murder of his child rather than that of his wife, he was given a free and posthumous pardon (see plate 25). His remains were exhumed and returned to his family. Still bearing the taint of being a killer, Evans was reburied, this time in a private grave rather than within the grounds of Pentonville prison. 10 Rillington Place, meanwhile, continued to be a tourist attraction for those of a ghoulish disposition, and John Christie stood alongside other notorious murderers in the Chamber of Horrors at Madame Tussaud's.

Interest in the case was revived in 1971 by the release of a film based on Kennedy's book. Richard Attenborough was suitably eerie as Christie and John Hurt, though taller and more robust than the real-life Evans, caught the Welshman's volatility and braggadocio. One of the most interesting performances was given by Pat Heywood as Ethel Christie, the long-suffering wife: to provide a motive for her murder, the film suggested that she had stopped sleeping with her husband and knew that he was involved in the death of Beryl Evans and her daughter. What made the film so effective was that it was shot in the very house where the crimes were committed. In a place as small and cluttered as this, tenants lived cheek by jowl, sharing a single lavatory, and coming and going through the same front door. It is easy to understand how, seeing an attractive young woman such as Beryl Evans so close every day, a man like Christie became obsessed with her: he was a voyeur, a photographer who peered through his lens at naked women, a midnight stalker, a master of the twitched curtain, a man who lit the fuse of his lust, then waited until it had burned to the point of explosion.

Later publications, however, advanced different interpretations of the case. One notable example was *Forty Years of Murder* by Professor Keith Simpson (1978). Simpson assisted in the exhumation of Beryl Evans and makes some pertinent comments, chiding Kennedy for his 'reckless over-statement' in claiming that, had a vaginal swab been taken from Beryl at the time, Dr Teare 'would almost certainly have found traces of Christie's spermatozoa'.

It was John Eddowes (son of Michael) who fully challenged the standard interpretation of the case. In *The Two Killers of Rillington Place* (1994), he is highly critical of Kennedy, arguing that Evans was a psychopath who killed his wife and child. As a result of threatened legal action by Kennedy, however, the first edition was withdrawn from sale.

The full truth of what happened at 10 Rillington Place on 8 November 1949 will never be known, but the cases of the two men continue to excite interest and debate. A recent fictional contribution to the literature is *Thirteen Steps Down* by Ruth Rendell (2005). Its protagonist, Mix Cellini, reveres Christie and has a small library of books about him; he is so obsessed with 10 Rillington Place that, even though the address no longer exists, he chooses to live near its original location in a decaying old house in Notting Hill. When he becomes fixated on a super-model living in the area, we get a chilling insight into the warped mind of a killer able to justify his horrific actions to himself.

John Christie was also able to justify his behaviour in his own mind. Showing no remorse, he talked about his victims (with the exception of his wife) with cool detachment. The closest he came to genuine regret was expressed the day before he was hanged, in a written request signed on 14 July 1953. 'The various photographs of my wife to be sent to Mrs. Bartle of 61 Hinde House Lane, Sheffield, together with my marriage certificate and an apology for any trouble I caused.'

The next day, this tormented man—who had tormented so many others—was no more.

Timothy John Evans was not the only innocent man to go to the gallows but, since capital punishment was abolished in the United Kingdom in 1965—partly because of reactions to his case—he was, thankfully, one of the last. In his encounter with one of the twentieth century's most appalling killers, this tragic, ineffectual little Welshman had made a larger contribution to history than was ever expected of him.

Sources & Reading

The National Archives holds extensive records relating to the Evans and Christie cases (some information is redacted), many of which are duplicates filed by different government departments. Some of the material is of a distressing nature.

Among several Metropolitan Police files, the main case files MEPO 2/9535 (Christie) and MEPO 3/3147 (Evans) include the original police statements made by the accused and by witnesses. MEPO 2/9535 also includes photographs.

The records of the Director of Public Prosecutions contain statements, exhibits (including photographs), trial transcripts and correspondence (Christie DPP 2/2246; Evans DPP 2/1927 and 1944). Some of this material is also in the files of the Central Criminal Court (e.g. CRIM 1/2035 on the Evans trial includes photographs).

The Prison Commission files PCOM 9/1668 (Christie) and PCOM 9/2313 (Evans) include medical reports, notes on the prisoner's history, and correspondence.

The Home Office files HO 291/227–8 duplicate much of the Christie prosecution evidence, including photographs. Files HO 45/24501–2 contain the material gathered in the course of Evans's rejected appeal in 1950. HO 45/25652–25662 document public pressure leading to the Brabin Inquiry and Evans's pardon. HO 299/18 and HO 282/52 concern the exhumation of Beryl Evans, and of her husband from prison grounds after his pardon.

The Cabinet Office collected and created extensive files on both cases during the Brabin Inquiry. These can be found in CAB 143/1–70 and include copies of witness statements, court exhibits, trial transcripts, correspondence, photographs and medical reports from the original prosecutions, as well as the documents relating to the Scott Henderson Inquiry. The Treasury Solicitor's Office also created extensive files at the time (TS 58/843–865).

For fuller information on National Archives' documents, search the catalogue at www.nationalarchives.gov.uk.

A number of books have been written on the case, including:

F.E. Camps, *Medical and Scientific Investigations in the Christie Case* (Medical Publications Ltd, 1953)

F.E. Camps and R. Barber, *The Investigation of Murder* (Scientific Book Club, 1966)

John Eddowes, *The Two Killers of Rillington Place* (Little, Brown, 1994)

M. Eddowes, *The Man On Your Conscience* (Cassell, 1955)

F. Tennyson Jesse (ed.), *The Trials of Timothy John Evans and John Reginald Halliday Christie* (Notable Trials series, William Hodge, 1957)

L. Kennedy, *10 Rillington Place* (Victor Gollancz, 1961)

R. Maxwell, *The Christie Case* (Gaywood Press, 1953)

R. Rendell, *Thirteen Steps Down* (Hutchinson, 2004)

K. Simpson, *Forty Years of Murder* (Harrap, 1978)

AUTHOR'S ACKNOWLEDGEMENTS

This book is dedicated to Sheila Knight, my perceptive and tenacious editor at the National Archives, to acknowledge the help and encouragement she has given me. I would also like to thank other members of staff for the unfailing friendliness and co-operation they showed during my visits.

PICTURE ACKNOWLEDGEMENTS

Pictures can be seen at the National Archives unless another source is given here. **1** Mirrorpix **4, 9** © Popperfoto/Alamy **19** © Bettmann/CORBIS

Index